A Guide To Therapeutic Child Care

A Guide to Therapeutic Child Care

What You Need to Know to Create a Healing Home

Ruth Emond, Laura Steckley and Autumn Roesch-Marsh

Jessica Kingsley *Publishers*
London and Philadelphia

First published in 2016
by Jessica Kingsley Publishers
73 Collier Street
London N1 9BE, UK
and
400 Market Street, Suite 400
Philadelphia, PA 19106, USA

www.jkp.com

Library of Congress Cataloging in Publication Data
Names: Emond, Ruth, author. | Steckley, Laura, author. | Roesch-Marsh,
  Autumn, author.
Title: A guide to therapeutic child care : what you need to know to create a
  healing home / Ruth Emond, Laura Steckley and Autumn Roesch-Marsh.
Description: London ;Philadelphia : Jessica Kingsley Publishers, 2016. |
  Includes bibliographical references and index.
Identifiers: LCCN 2015027457 | ISBN 9781849054010 (alk. paper)
Subjects: LCSH: Psychic trauma in children-Treatment. | Parent and child.
Classification: LCC RJ506.P66 E47 2016 | DDC
618.92/8521--dc23 LC record available at
http://lccn.loc.gov/2015027457

British Library Cataloguing in Publication Data
A CIP catalogue record for this book is available from the British Library

ISBN 978 1 84905 401 0
eISBN 978 0 85700 769 8

Printed and bound in Great Britain

Contents

I

Introduction

This book is a celebration of the remarkable care that is being given to children, every day. It also highlights how incredible children and young people are at letting adults know what they need and want. The book grew out of our experiences of working with children who are looked after away from home as well as supporting, researching and learning from foster carers, residential staff and adoptive parents. What we share is a passionate belief that everyday experiences shape children's sense of themselves and that such everyday experiences hold enormous therapeutic potential. Throughout the book we argue that daily life has the power to soothe, to hold and to repair. When this is allowed to happen within the context of 'home', the richness of these experiences is increased.

We have had the privilege of working with some incredible carers and staff who have shared with us their experiences, feelings and hopes. We have also drawn on our own practice with children and young people. In sharing these experiences with you, we have tried to be honest about the range of emotions, the frustrations, disappointments, joys and elations that these relationships and experiences have provided us with. Over the year that we have worked together on the book, we have found ourselves talking about and remembering so many wonderful children and carers. We have thought about how our own practice has changed over time and how we are increasingly convinced that what happens in the *everyday* world of children makes the difference.

Home within the context of this book is the place where we should feel safe; it should be a harbour from the choppy seas of life and where we can truly be ourselves. However, this soothing utopia of a safe, comfortable and peaceful home may, at times, seem a million miles from the busy family homes or residential units where many of us live and work. While it is true that the behaviour of children and adults may make it difficult to achieve the peace and calm we aspire to, we think that what really makes a home a place of healing is the extent to which the pain that is brought into the home is accepted and kept readily to mind by the people providing the care. By holding in mind the past that the child brings to you, attention will always be on how changes to the daily routine or world around the child can help them to recover.

For a healing environment to be created, those who are providing that wonderful day-to-day care need also to be cared for. The hurt caused by living with the past needs to be acknowledged and repaired for them too. This book considers the experience of the carers as well as the child and offers ways to think about what both need to maintain a safe and nurturing home. It can be useful to think of healing environments as made up like Russian dolls, with many layers that are important to the whole. The child in the centre needs to have the loving containment of the adult providing his care. The adult providing that care also needs to be emotionally held and practically supported by another (manager, partner, social worker). In order to continue to provide support in a meaningful way, that support person too needs to be offered assistance by their organisation and so on. Providing healing care takes it out of us, whatever place we hold in the circles around the child. Care and attention needs to be given to people at all levels.

Underpinning much of the book are the very powerful feelings that healing homes create and contain. The children who we care for often come to us filled with fear: fear created by past hurts, harms and disappointments, but also fear of what the future will bring and what your care will offer. By being cared for, by eventually receiving and giving love, these children's lives will change. And change in and of itself creates fear.

For those who look after children who have been traumatised by the past, the tensions between fear and love are also present. Many residential child care workers and foster carers have talked with us about their fear of not being able to manage, of letting the child down, of being seen as not able or not good enough. Fear can also come from falling in love with the child they are caring for. Is love 'allowed' between carer and child? Will the child reject their love or be moved on?

Looking after children who have been removed from birth parents as a result of trauma, whether as foster carer, residential staff member or adoptive parent, brings with it many elements of day-to-day life that are shared by birth parents. However, what makes this parenting different is that as carers or parents you are not only dealing with the here and now experience your child is having, but also the way in which the past has shaped it. The past is never far away from us and if that past has been filled with terror, uncertainty, confusion and hopelessness, as 'substitute' parents, we have to be mindful of how our parenting manages not only the present but gives account of, and goes some way to help soothe, the past. We hope this book will give you some tools to make sense of the impact the past can have on the present and some practical strategies you can use to create a healing home.

We decided to write in a way that allows the reader to dip in and out of the book. You don't need to read it from front to back. Instead it is laid out in discrete chapters, which we hope will offer some up-to-date thinking and research around different aspects of day-to-day life. We've provided some additional reading and suggestions for resources to allow you to follow your interest in each of the topics covered.

Each chapter includes sections on what you might notice in your child, how you might feel, what you and others can do to help, as well as things you might like to try. The 'things you might like to try' are not a list of magic bullets (unfortunately) and, like most interventions, they don't so much rely on what you do, but *how* you do it. What you feel, both at the time of undertaking the activities, as well as about the suggestions more generally will significantly impact on their effectiveness. We encourage you to look for opportunities where these strategies or suggestions might be useful in an everyday way. Many will need to be practised, rehearsed or thought about in advance. They have to feel helpful to you and give you a sense that they 'fit' with how you want to support your child. It may well be that you don't like them all or that they don't match with how you want to care for your child, or you may want to change or alter them to a way that better suits your style and approach. Keeping an open mind and heart is what matters here.

You'll see that the chapters also include 'Spotlights on Practice' where examples from our own work or experience shared with us are included, as well as some questions or activities to help you think about how these issues might relate to you and your child. You may want to use these 'Pause for Reflection' exercises and 'Things to Try' suggestions in supervision or team discussions.

We should alert you to some of the decisions we made about language. To try to make the reading of each chapter flow, you will see that the child or young person is either written as male or female. We did this because it made 'the child' at the centre of our discussions more present. However, the points being raised are relevant to both boys and girls. This book is primarily concerned with children who have experienced pain as a result of the actions of primary carers. Whilst aspects of the book consider what might lead to the obstacles facing adults in being the parents their child needs them to be, this is not looked at in detail. Similarly, whilst we consider some of the ways in which our actions as carers can better support children who have not only experienced neglect and abuse but who also have additional support needs or who have a disability, we would hope that many of the points made translate across the range of childhoods and children that we care for. Home is used alongside the terms unit or children's unit. Again, many of the suggestions and reflections apply to all settings where children are looked after. We also made the decision to use the word 'carer'. In most cases this term covers anyone providing everyday care of a child, be that short-term or permanent foster carers, residential workers or those embarking on preparation work to become adoptive parents. However, we hope that this book will also be useful to those involved in the indirect care of children, including social workers, team managers, supervising social workers/support staff and specialist therapists.

The stories contained in the book reflect real experiences that we have had or have had shared with us. We are grateful to those who gave permission and have made every effort to anonymise both these stories and the ones relating to children who we can no longer trace to gain permission. We so enjoyed thinking and talking about these children again.

This book is not just about creating a healing home for children; it's also about creating a healing home for all the people who live in it. That includes you! We want to highlight and share the wonderful work that your colleagues and fellow carers are doing, showing the everyday practice that is otherwise invisible. We hope that you will be as inspired as we have been listening and gathering together these experiences. Caring for children who have past hurts can be a lonely and painful experience. It can also be full of joy and wonder. We hope that we have captured this in the book and that you will find something in here that assures you of your good work and encourages the changes you want to make. In your informed efforts are the keys for creating a healing home.

2

The Developing Person

Introduction: What is human development?

It was like, 'woah, I don't do o-logy. That's an o-logy thing.' But actually once I got my head around it, it made sense and it kind of helped me understand… I became quite excited by my knowledge and wanting to share that…the whole of my practice has changed, and probably my attitude as well.

(Residential worker speaking in a research interview about her experiences of learning)

Developmental theory covers a vast range of research and approaches to understanding what makes us who we are. It is about exploring the processes of change that human beings go through throughout their lives. Increasingly, developmental theories recognise that how we grow and change is influenced by the world around us, both in terms of how we interact with and experience that world, as well as how, in turn, it experiences and reacts to us. In this sense, human development is a dynamic process: the environment shapes and is shaped by the individuals within it, past, present and future.

This chapter gives an overview of human development, with a particular focus on children and young people. As you can imagine, there isn't the space to cover all of this in one chapter. Instead, what we want to do is introduce you to some of the key ideas that will be revisited throughout the book. For some of you, this will be very much a refresher course, whilst for others these ways of understanding your own and your child's development will be new.

It begins with a brief look at some of the significant influences on development, the different aspects of development and ways of understanding it. Many of the children who we care for have encountered experiences in which their physical, emotional, social and cognitive development has not been well supported. Some of the problems that can result are touched on in the chapter, as well as key theoretical terms used to explain or explore these difficulties. This leads us to thinking about why it is important for parents and carers to know something about developmental theory. Finally, we give examples of how these ideas might help in your caring role.

The chapter is not intended to provide you with all you need to know about human and child development. Instead, we hope that you will find our introduction to the topic and key concepts a useful starting point for further exploration and learning. We also hope to begin to answer some questions that carers often raise, like:

Why is developmental theory important for caring?

What are some of the important concepts that can help me understand a child's development?

How do I know whether behaviour is part of normal development or something else?

How can developmental theory help me to know myself better?

Influences on development

You are one of the most significant influences on the ongoing development of the child in your care. You will be doing much of the vital work of making sense of the world for her. It is to you that she will look to gain a sense of who she is and how the world works (although it might not always feel like that!). This is no easy task as often children will bring with them the previous ways that they have been taught to understand. For many, this will be a very different perspective on both the world around them and on themselves as individuals.

Although you are one of the most significant environmental factors, it is important to understand that development is a multi-dimensional process, which means that many things influence the process of change and growth across the lifespan. The diagram below outlines the key influences including: biological influences, social processes, structural systems and culture. It is important to remember that many of these factors are inter-related; for example, social processes are influenced by culture and systems.

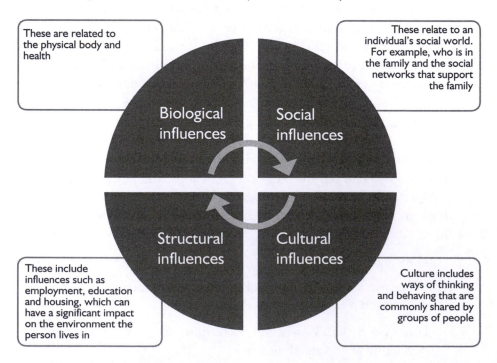

Figure 2.1 Developmental influences

Stages of development

Much of what is written about development focuses on key stages of human growth. There is considerable debate among researchers and theorists about the precise parameters and developmental tasks of each stage. However, the key stages that are included in many overviews are presented in Table 2.1.

Table 2.1 Developmental stages

Stage	Age	Developmental tasks
Prenatal	From conception to birth	• The human foetus goes through a rapid set of biological developmental stages over a typical period of 9 months • The health of the mother has a significant impact on the progress of growth • Start of relationship with self and others
Infancy and toddlerhood	From birth to 2 years	• Attachments to primary caregivers • Infant begins to develop ways of organising the world • Growing connections between what is seen, heard and touched (sensory) and producing a body response (motor) • Emotional development (includes beginning to recognise feelings in others)
Early childhood	2 years to 6 years	• Developing more motor skills • Language development (including language for feelings) • Fantasy play and later peer play • Beginning to develop greater self-control • Beginning to recognise differences between genders and identify with one or other • Early moral development • Beginning to develop a sense of own self

cont.

Stage	Age	Developmental tasks
Later childhood	6 years to 12 years	• Friendships • Development of logical and rule-based thinking • Skill learning • Self-evaluation • Team play
Adolescence	12 years to 20 years	• Physical maturation (including puberty) • Becoming more confident in abstract thinking • Growing emotional development • Membership in the peer group • Sexual relationships • Autonomy from parents • Gender identity • Internalised morality • Career choice • Development of identity/ experimentation with identity
Early adulthood	20 years to 35 years	• Exploring intimate relationships • Childbearing • Work • Lifestyle • Changing identity
Middle adulthood	35 years to 65 years	• Managing a career • Nurturing an intimate relationship • Expanding caring relationships • Managing the household • Menopause
Late adulthood	65 years to end of life	• Accepting one's life • Redirecting energy towards new roles and activities • Promoting intellectual vigour • Developing a point of view about death • Coping with physical changes in ageing • Travelling through unchartered terrain

Adapted from Harms (2005)

At each stage of life there are core developmental tasks. A number of theorists argue that the way in which we experience each stage shapes subsequent stages. These stages are often linked to particular developmental milestones, such as learning to walk or the onset of puberty. Some of these milestones relate to biological changes like the physical growth of the body and changes in hormones. However, they also relate to particular emotional and psychological processes that help shape our inner world. For example, our sense that we are loved and that caring adults will meet our needs reflects our early experiences of being loved and cared for. Others are more closely linked to socially determined milestones, for example, going to school or leaving home. These vary according to the social and cultural context; in some cultures, children might enter adulthood at a much earlier age than others due to different cultural norms around marriage and expectations about starting a family. Historical and structural changes can also impact on these stages. For example, in some social groups, young adults leave home later due to the rising costs of housing and higher education.

In order to best support your child, it is important to have a sense of which developmental tasks are occurring at each stage and to work with social workers, birth families, teachers and health professionals to create a picture of what in your child's development is 'ordinary' and what might be considered 'extra ordinary'. It is only by having a good sense of the 'ordinary' that you will be able to do this.

Knowing what to expect at each stage of the life course is important for carers. It helps us to make sense of the actions and behaviours of the children we care for, to know what they need at each stage and to guide our parenting and caregiving practices. Carers are also at their own stage in the life course and will have had their unique journey to this point. So, your own age and stage also matter and will likely impact on how you view and understand the child and her needs, as well as your experience of caregiving.

Pause for Reflection

In thinking about a child you care for, what are some of the influences on her development from each of the four areas depicted in Figure 2.1? Looking at each of the developmental stages in turn, how did these influences affect the stages outlined in Table 2.1? What about your own developmental journey? What do you think has influenced how you have experienced each life stage?

Domains of development

Throughout life, aspects of the individual grow and change in a variety of ways. Often these are described as 'domains'. Traditionally, researchers have tended to focus on one particular developmental domain, often in isolation from the others. In recent times, the links between fields of research have improved to deepen our understanding of human behaviour. A similar shift has happened amongst the various professionals involved with looked-after children, and health, education and social work professionals are more likely to share information and resources and to contribute to both the assessment and support of children in looked-after care. However, it is important to note that each professional will have different levels of expertise relating to each of the domains and will be assessing your child from their professional perspective. Most commonly the areas considered in developmental research and practice are:

Physical: development of the brain and body, fine and gross motor skills (coordination) and the senses

Spiritual: the development of a sense of meaning, broader purpose, awe, wonder and connectedness with the world. Can be located in religious practices, but not necessarily

Cognitive: development of learning, problem solving, understanding, abstract thinking, ethical reasoning

Domains of development

Emotional: development of understanding of feelings, ways of expressing them, capacity to manage them; development of attunement and empathy

Social: development of relationships, identity, understanding of others' motivations and feelings, social skills

Figure 2.2 Domains of development

Spotlight on practice

Billy was 6 when Ruth started to work with him. He had experienced chronic physical and emotional neglect when he was living with his birth parents. He had been removed from their care when he was 5 and placed with foster carers, Amy and Chris. Since living with them, Billy had made significant developmental progress across all domains. However, in one of the sessions with Ruth, Billy talked about his struggles to play with the other boys. As he talked, it appeared that the boys in his class wanted to play football.

He said that the ball always came to him too fast and that he couldn't kick it back. Prior to coming to live with Amy and Chris, Billy had had very little support in developing gross motor skills. Clearly, the impact of this physical challenge was also contributing to Billy's social development (he felt unable to participate, describing himself as 'weird') as well as emotionally (the feelings of shame and isolation were experienced as 'his fault' rather than as a result of the boys not being willing to play something else). Amy and Chris were not physically active or able to play football with him. This meant that he didn't have anyone at home who could help him 'catch up' with some of the developmental opportunities he had missed out on.

Events like this occur every day for lots of children and, for many, they will have had a robust enough developmental foundation to make sense of the responses by peers and understand that it is not their fault. They may also have supportive adults to help them to do so and to help them find alternative ways to cope, other games to play or opportunities to develop the skills they want to attain. As Billy's example highlights, developmental domains don't just overlap or connect in the here and now; in addition, the previous experiences an individual has had in each of these domains also play a significant part in the current experience.

What happens within each of the five developmental domains depends on age, previous developmental experiences and the social, emotional and physical environment that an individual is exposed to. The pace and rate of change and growth varies enormously from one child to the next, and for carers it can be a struggle to balance parental fears of what is developmentally 'abnormal' and the 'norm' for what might be expected of the child at that point in the life course. Developmental changes rarely take place in a predictable way. Indeed, children often go from periods of appearing 'stuck' to making huge jumps in physical, emotional, cognitive and social development.

In addition, developmental change can occur at different rates within each of the domains. Some children you care for may appear younger emotionally, socially, cognitively and/or even physically than their chronological age. For example, you might have witnessed social and emotional behaviour reminiscent of a 2-year-old coming from a child who is chronologically 14. You will also probably know that simply telling the 14 year old to 'grow up' or 'act his age' is of no benefit. It usually makes things worse, and in fact is no different from telling a 14 year old who is physically small due to neglect to 'be taller'.

As has been mentioned already in the chapter, it is important for those caring for and working with looked-after children to know what might be expected for children at each stage and in each of the domains. This not only helps to identify potential developmental challenges or gaps ('the extra ordinary'), but also prevents us from expecting too much from children before they have the physical, emotional or cognitive capacity to deliver it.

Crucially, having knowledge of 'normal' development can also limit otherwise 'normal' behaviours being labelled as 'abnormal'. This knowledge is something that can be drawn on, over and over again. For example, in work with foster and kinship carers, Ruth has found it helpful to begin by reviewing the 'norms' of development for the age of the child who is being cared for. Usually, Ruth reads this with the carers as she too can't hold in her head all of the different information across the domains. This work helps to free Ruth and the carers from relying solely on their own experiences of children to make their assessment of the child, and helps ground them in what might be 'normal' to expect to see. One of the books Ruth uses to do this is Vera Fahlberg's (2012) *A Child's Journey through Placement*. It includes a great chapter outlining 'normal' development at each stage and is written in an accessible and detailed way. We have included it in the 'Further reading' section at the end of the chapter.

Pause for Reflection

Are there areas of your child's development where you're unsure about what's normal and what's a cause for concern? Which domain(s) might this development fall within?

Lenses on development

Not only do theorists have different opinions about which domains are more or less important, there are also many lenses or perspectives that researchers and professionals might look through to understand your child. There are endless explanations for why human beings behave as they do but, in general terms, these can be split into a number of key perspectives, as outlined in Figure 2.3.

Figure 2.3 Lenses on development

As you might expect, these views on why people behave as they do place differing emphasis on each of the domains. As you read through this book, you will see that many of the approaches that we have taken to understanding children and your relationship with them come from both a psychodynamic and a psychosocial perspective. These two approaches stress the importance of the impact of previous life stages on the development of a sense of self and relationship with the external world. They accept that not all actions and thoughts take place in the conscious mind; indeed, they place great store in the role of the unconscious. However, these models of understanding acknowledge the environment around the individual and seek to explore and make sense of how this environmental context shapes and is shaped by the individual.

Core concepts

There are several core concepts that will help you to make sense of your child's development and of some of the content in this book. Much of what we have written so far in this chapter refers to **stage theories**. This collection of ideas spans a range of disciplines and approaches, but common to them all is the belief that development occurs incrementally and that at different points in life we are preoccupied by achieving a range of different tasks. One way of thinking about this is to view life as a ladder. Each life stage represents a rung on the ladder and our experience of going up the ladder will be shaped by how we've got to our current rung. Theorists vary as to the role that environment plays in the experience of life stages; however, there is a growing body of work which suggests that our biological and physical selves are heavily influenced by the experiences that we have throughout life and the social and environmental context that has surrounded us. This is important as it suggests that, whilst early trauma may have had a significant impact on an individual across the five domains, the body, brain and social self are able to make, at least some, recovery.

Thinking about stages of life is important for carers as often we are caring for children who have missed out on 'optimal conditions for growth'. Indeed, there may have been experiences in their lives that acted to prevent or inhibit growth and development. As a result, we may be looking after children whose chronological age is not matched by their physical, emotional, social or cognitive stage of development. For some children, this mismatch is present in most of their day-to-day experiences, whilst for others, it is at times of anxiety and uncertainty that they are pulled back to earlier emotional and social states. Some theorists refer to this as **regression**. This way of behaving (retreating to an earlier stage) is not a decision made consciously by a child but rather is something that happens as a means of protection, a 'safer' place to be. Carers therefore need to know not only what to expect given the child's chronological age, but also about the child's progress through previous stages and how to respond to earlier stage behaviour.

In the course of this book, we will look at a range of ways that carers can support children to recover from past hurt or make up for developmental experiences that may have been absent from their lives. Central to these approaches is what might be referred to as **reflective parenting**. This approach to caring for a child places at the centre the role of parents in bearing witness to the thoughts, actions and beliefs of a child, acting as a container or psychological carrier of these and being able to reflect back to the child what has been shared. In other words, the parent not only notices her child's emotions and anxieties, but psychologically holds onto them and reflects them back to the child in a way that is manageable. This process is sometimes called **containment**. Chapter Four deals with how this way of caring for children helps them to learn to use thinking to manage their own powerful feelings in a way that is not overwhelming. Containment is an 'ordinary' aspect of good enough parenting, but for many of the children that we care for, it will be a very new experience. Often it is this capacity to work with containment that indicates the ability of caregivers to provide children with what they need. Reflective parenting and containment are perhaps best illustrated by an example.

Spotlight on Practice

Jamie returned from school angry and upset. As he entered the house, he threw his bag on the ground and announced that he hated school. His carer, Pete, acknowledged this powerful entrance 'Wow, you've had a really tough day. You're REALLY upset about school.' (Here Pete is bearing witness to what Jamie is presenting – he is seeing, hearing and feeling what Jamie has to say.) Jamie replies with 'I hate it and I'm not going back.' Pete sees that Jamie is close to tears although is presenting as angry and so says: 'This is really hard for you, you're really sad and upset.' As he does this, Pete takes Jamie's bag and hangs it up. (In these actions, Pete is accepting and containing Jamie's actions, thoughts and beliefs. He is not at this point trying to correct them or dismiss them.) Jamie is able to calm a little. Pete goes on: '…it sounds like something went wrong for you today and you don't know what to do next'. (This reflection of what Pete has experienced helps Jamie know that he is not alone with his feelings and that Pete is going to be alongside him.) From this point, they are able to talk together about what really happened.

Whilst the above example is brief, it highlights the importance of trying to see the world from the child's view. This doesn't mean that the child is 'right' or that you have to collude with 'bad' behaviour. Rather, by taking as your starting point an attempt to see, hear and feel what the child has experienced, you are not only offering a reparative experience of warm, nurturing parenting (which many children in alternative care may have missed in their earlier life), you are also holding the child's feelings until she is able to manage them. You can imagine how this scenario would have gone if Pete had replied, 'Don't you talk to me like that. Go up to your room and change out of your school clothes.' Rather than being emotionally held and contained, Jamie would have felt further rejected and 'bad'.

There is a growing body of work that suggests children's very early experiences of being noticed and responded to have a fundamental impact on how they come to understand themselves as well as their relationships with others. These responses are especially important at times of stress and distress. Having an attuned parent, one who notices our stress and is able to comfort us in ways that become predictable and satisfying, is the basis of security and trust in the self and in the external world. One way in which this has been understood is **attachment theory**. Attachment is more than just a close relationship; it is a system of behaviours – signals and cues – that all infants use to bring carers close and to get their needs met. Our attachment systems enabled us to survive. As carers, attachment theory helps us to know that early experiences create an unconscious template for relationships (both with self and others) and understand that children bring these templates or maps of relationships into their relationships with us. This has been called the child's **internal working model** of relationships. We too have an internal working model that guides our behaviour in relationships and shapes what we might expect from others. As carers, our internal working model and the internal working model belonging to the child we care for can sometimes be at odds. For instance, you may have looked after a child who understood your acts of kindness as 'trickery' or a precursor to harm. Another example would be experiencing a child's constant touching or following of us as 'creepy' or suffocating, whilst for her it has been the way to elicit contact or appease adults.

These feelings can be **conscious** to us, in that we may be aware of what we are thinking and feeling and why that is. However, when it comes to relationships, very often, our responses are shaped by our **unconscious** mind. The meaning of these two terms has caused great theoretical debate within a range of academic and clinical disciplines. Within the context of this book, we use these terms to describe the part of our self which we are aware of and which we can readily seek answers from (the conscious mind), and that deeper part of our personality which stores many of our own childhood feelings and memories, the parts of us which are harder to access or make sense of, but which drive many of our behaviours and interpretations of the world (the unconscious mind).

This way of understanding the self is important for carers, as often we want to ask 'why' of the child and can be frustrated by what seems to be the genuine response of 'I don't know'. Similarly, we can feel shocked or confused by our responses to behaviours or situations and unable to establish why we responded as we did. Safe exploration of these experiences needs to be available for the child and for the carer in order to move forward. Deepening our understanding of our own and the child's **inner world** is important to ensure that our interventions and ways of caring are the most appropriate for the child and for us as carers. This inner world refers to internal experiences (conscious and unconscious) of values, feelings, thoughts and fantasies; it is the place where we have our relationship with ourselves. For many of the children we look after, their inner world has required strong protection and has undergone significant attack from the external environment. We must therefore allow the children to dictate the pace at which they are able to let us get closer to this inner self.

For all of the children we have cared for there will be experiences of *loss*, *grief* and *mourning*. At the very least, children will have lost their previous way of living with whomever their caregivers once were. For most, the experience of **ambiguous loss**, of losing someone but knowing that they are still out there and may return or be found, has a profound impact. Children need to be supported in exploring the range of feelings and memories that they have of those people, places and things that have been lost, and carers need to be supported to work with deep and painful loss which can endure for the child long after the move into placement. In particular, many theories would suggest that feelings of loss are re-experienced with every new loss. New loss can be an everyday event, from leaving you to go to school, to changing activity in the classroom, to having outgrown clothes. If the child hasn't been able to make sense of and recover from losses, she will have greater difficulties managing the everyday small losses.

Loss can also be a feature of the experience for us as carers. We may feel a sense of grief for the child or the family that we thought that we might have. As we begin to know ourselves as parents or carers, we may need to grieve for the parent we thought we would be. Many of the carers we have worked with have described the differences between the expected experiences of looking after children and the reality. Sometimes, this can concern the impact past trauma has had, for others it can be a growing awareness of the impact disability or additional support needs will have on the child in the long term. Understanding loss and grief can be a key to unlock our responses and feelings as well as those of the children we care for. They too may be grieving for the parents or carers they had hoped for.

The loss we experience when children leave our care should not be underestimated. Even when a child leaves our care under positive circumstances, we (and they) are still losing the relationship as it was. When a child leaves our care under difficult circumstances, feelings of loss can be compounded by a sense of failure or loss of hope for making things work. In addition, caring for many children increases the number of losses we will experience. There are, of course, many things we gain from our time caring for children, but the nature and experience of loss related to alternative care settings rarely gets discussed or acknowledged. We think it is important to do so.

How quickly many of us forget the monumental loss and change that our children have encountered, the impact of which is not tempered by young age. Indeed, more recent research has suggested that children are more likely to recover from loss if they are in middle to late childhood and adolescence rather than at earlier stages of development. Previously, many had thought that the younger the child, the lesser the impact. However, such children are often left with no one to help them make sense of what had happened to them and have yet to develop the cognitive, social and emotional skills to do so for themselves. Similarly, there has been a lack of recognition of the needs of children with communication or cognitive disabilities in relation to the impact of loss and change.

Interestingly, some writers in the field of child development stress that a sense of loss occurs for children and carers/parents as each developmental milestone is achieved. This may not be experienced at a conscious level, but growth in each of these domains creates change in a child's world. For some, this can generate feelings of anxiety or trigger loss experiences.

It can be helpful to recognise significant times of **transition** for children and young people which may trigger feelings of loss or anxiety. Transitions may relate to developmental milestones or may be triggered by other significant changes, like moving school or placement. Even when changes like moving house are abrupt, most transitions don't happen overnight. This is because transition is a process. Many children and young people who we have worked with have had many unsupported transitions in their lives. They have not been provided with security and continuity of relationships, making transitions painful and in some cases re-traumatising, as they are reminded of previous losses. In order to support children with a transition we first need to recognise it as such. We then need to seek to understand what this transition means to this child and help to manage their fears and anxieties. As young people approach the period of leaving care, this is an especially important task. We should plan well ahead and work with others in the young person's support network to provide as much continuity of relationships and other supports as possible. Throughout this book we will reflect on the emotional needs of children during times of change and transition and provide further suggestions about how you might understand and respond to what they are going through.

Finally, the core concept of **resilience** is very useful in thinking about how to support children's development. Resilience refers to the phenomenon of developing well or even thriving under adverse circumstances. Most of this book focuses on ways of developing environments that cultivate children and young people's resilience.

Why is knowing about development important?

In caring for children and young people, our fundamental goals are to support their growth and to help them to flourish. Understanding *how* children grow gives us some direction in *what* to do to support them. An analogy can be made with growing houseplants. Knowing that plants need light, that some need direct sun whilst others need to be protected from it, that all need water but in differing amounts and frequency makes us more successful at maintaining a home full of thriving plants. When a plant gets tall and 'leggy', it's telling us that it needs more light. If its leaves droop, we have probably waited too long to water it. Similarly, understanding what each individual child needs in order to thrive, and being able to interpret some of the coded ways that children tell us they haven't got what they need, helps us to foster their growth.

You don't have to be a botanist or a microbiologist to have green fingers, and similarly, you don't have to become a professor of child development to be an expert carer. But as with plants, some knowledge is necessary. An understanding of some of the core ideas contained within developmental theory will go a very long way in helping to navigate the complexities that children bring us and to meeting their needs. Developmental theory can help us to have more realistic expectations of children and young people, and to better understand behaviours that relate to a developmental task or struggle.

Spotlight on Practice

Dan had Theresa, a toddler he is fostering, with him at the garden centre, and he had his hands full. Theresa was romping about getting her hands into everything while Dan was trying to decide which bedding plants to choose for the front garden. He was getting increasingly frustrated. In his attempts to get her to stop, he would frequently squat down and try to talk and reason with her, giving long explanations for why she should do as he asked. He was trying to be a good dad, but the strain on his patience could be heard in his voice and his frustration was mounting. It just wasn't working.

From a developmental perspective, we know that toddlers are often compelled to explore the world around them and in so doing want to touch everything. You could call it their job at that age. We know that toddlers' ability to reason is not yet developed, and that they have short attention spans. So we can see why Dan's approach wasn't working. His expectations, both of her behaviour and of her ability to respond to his attempts to reason with her, weren't based in the reality of where she was developmentally.

The example of Dan in the garden centre could be representative of any parent. Recognising the developmental stage that our child is at helps us remain aware of what she is able to do and to understand what her developmental stage leads her to focus on. As many of us know, this is not always easy.

However, in addition to understanding what all children need in order to flourish, foster and residential carers and adoptive parents also need to have an understanding of the potential impact of trauma and other adverse experiences on development. Coming to appreciate how experience of separation, neglect, abuse or other trauma affects a child's development, rather than just 'how it affected the child', can shift thinking in important ways. Instead of seeing the child as inherently damaged or problematic, we can more usefully focus on aspects of previous care that were interrupted or even side-tracked. For example, thinking again about Theresa, if she were highly anxious or frightened (or what might be described, clinically, as in a state of 'heightened arousal') due to, for example, the signals from her empty tummy, she would no longer be able to explore her world in the same way – to reach out and grasp things, to meet her carer, Dan, with her smiling eyes, to feel and smell the soil and flowers. These normal infant behaviours are necessary for her to develop – physically, cognitively and emotionally.

In the short term, these interruptions have little developmental impact but Theresa may have been removed from a home life where this heightened arousal due to hunger, fear, discomfort or pain became a chronic state of affairs for her. Long term, the frequent inability to engage in exploratory behaviours will be likely to delay her physical, cognitive and emotional development. It may also promote her development in other ways – ways that may enable her to survive her environment but may also cause problems when she has to manage other environments. For instance, her exaggerated expressions of distress may have been necessary to garner a parent's attention at home, but it may alienate her peers and interrupt her learning when she goes to school.

When our orientation shifts from a focus on the 'damaged' child to the child who missed out on important caring processes, the healing power of the everyday comes into clearer focus. It is all the seemingly small, caring acts that, when accumulated over time, actually make the difference in a child's life. Your understanding of the impact of trauma and other adversities gives you important information about the kinds of caring processes that are needed by the children or young people in your home or residential unit.

Such understanding can also help you to have realistic expectations for a child who has experienced them, and also for the process of recovery. Jack Phelan, a former carer in residential settings, and now an educator of carers, offers a useful term for thinking about what happens for some children: 'developmental stuckness' – a child can get stuck, developmentally, if she doesn't have the necessary help to let go of survival behaviours that are now getting in the way of her development. This can often lead to a vicious cycle.

More often than not, interruptions to development, and all the hurt that came with them, happened incrementally. Healing and recovery, healthy development and thriving will come about incrementally too. This may be the most important way that a developmental orientation can inform your expectations. Consider the number of caring processes and interactions that happen in just a single day when all is going well in the life of an infant. Multiply this by 365, and that's the number needed in just the first year of life – for a healthy infant in a healthy setting. The number of caring processes necessary when things have gone poorly may be far greater. It takes time and repetition.

Pause for Reflection

Are there ways that a child you care for is developmentally 'stuck'? How does he or she show you this?

What threatens development?

It may be helpful to organise threats to children's development into two categories: intrinsic and extrinsic. Intrinsic refers to the characteristics of the child, and extrinsic are the characteristics of her environment. When the internal characteristics raise the likelihood of problems with development, they can be termed as vulnerabilities; threats from the environment are often called adversities. This way of thinking about threats to development is very well explained in a book called *Child Development for Child Care and Protection Workers* (Daniel *et al.* 2010) and we have given further details about it in our 'Further reading' section.

Of course, the internal and external affect one another. For example, poor experiences of attachment and an internal working model that sees all adults as a threat will be internal characteristics of vulnerability in a child. A chaotic and threatening environment in which the parents are too caught up in their own difficulties to consistently provide safety and care would be external characteristics, or adversities. Another layer in this example might include parental poverty and addiction in a community where there is limited access to good related services – further adversities coming from outside the family. Considering the intrinsic and extrinsic – the vulnerabilities and the adversities – enables the identification of where help is best targeted. It is also keeps us mindful that a child may be developmentally stuck as a result of a complicated web of factors; it's never just down to the family or simply the immaturity of the child.

Before offering some examples of vulnerabilities and adversities, we want to make a couple of provisos. First, not all threats to healthy development necessarily interrupt development or cause a child to be developmentally stuck. Sometimes the strengths in the child and the strengths in her environment cushion the negative effects of the threats, and her development stays more or less on track. As mentioned above, this is referred to as resilience. Second, the use of the word 'vulnerability' in relation to developmental threats does not mean that being vulnerable is a bad thing. We all need to be vulnerable to a certain degree to have closeness in our relationships. Indeed, allowing ourselves to be vulnerable in certain circumstances can be an important strength. Also, it is important not to equate vulnerability with weakness. For example, belonging to a minority ethnic group is a potential vulnerability for many children. While their ethnicity is clearly an intrinsic characteristic, it is just as clear that the racism in the culture round about them is the extrinsic threat to development. Indeed, if a child's ethnic community is healthy and strong, her ethnicity may simultaneously be a strength and a vulnerability. It is in the interplay between the intrinsic and the extrinsic where we can most clearly see the threats (and supports) for children's development. This example also highlights that when we stop seeing vulnerabilities as weaknesses, we are more able to see the strengths that are sometimes bound up in them.

Whilst there are too many intrinsic characteristics to list them all here, the book mentioned above and listed in the 'Further reading' section below is a good place to read about more of them (Daniel *et al.* 2010). Here we simply offer a few to give you a sense of those characteristics that are associated with vulnerability: an infant who is born prematurely or who has a condition that makes it very difficult for her to accept comfort and settle; a toddler who has no impulse control; an adolescent who hasn't yet developed good social skills and has difficulty making and keeping friends. Many of the conditions currently labelled as 'disabilities' are considered under this framework as intrinsic characteristics. However, we would argue that as carers, we need to consider not only the impact of trauma and neglect on disability, but also the way in which the external world responds to the needs and differences of individuals. This leads us to extrinsic characteristics.

Similarly, extrinsic characteristics that threaten children's healthy development are many. Again, we encourage you to read up on this further but in the meantime, we offer just a few: stresses within a family, including parental mental health problems, addiction, domestic violence, one or both parents' poor experiences of attachment when they were children or unemployment; stresses on the family, including poverty, social exclusion and racism; and stresses on the community, including limited spaces for safe and enjoyable play, overstretched or poor services – both basic services (e.g. housing estates with local shops with no fresh food and poor access to public transport) and services aimed at providing added support – and schools with low levels of material and social investment.

All forms of abuse, whether physical, emotional, psychological or sexual, pose a significant threat to healthy development; neglect is also just as serious a threat. Two key considerations in making sense of the interplay of the intrinsic and extrinsic and the impact on development are the age of the child and the relationships she has and has had. The younger the child is when she encounters adversity or when her vulnerabilities become prominent, the greater the threat to her healthy development. Additionally, children who have few or no adult figures who consistently offer care and support and to whom they can turn to in times of need are at much greater risk of interrupted development.

Pause for Reflection

What are or were some of the threats to your child's development? Which ones do you have the most positive influence over? Which ones can be reduced more immediately and which ones will take time to affect? In what ways does the external world support or increase the impact of your child's disability and/or behaviours?

What supports development?

> *The greatest need of a child is to obtain conclusive assurance (a) that he is genuinely loved as a person by his parents and (b) that his parents genuinely accept his love...frustration of this desire to be loved as a person and to have his love accepted is the greatest trauma that a child can experience.*
>
> *(Fairbairn 1952, pp.39–40)*

There are many things that parents and carers can do to support or enhance the development of the children and young people they are looking after. In this section we will highlight some of the most important, but we will return to these and others throughout the book. It is important to think about your reflections concerning the developmental threats or gaps that your child has experienced. By doing this, you will not only think about your child at her current chronological age but also the stages she has had to navigate to get to this point.

The first thing any parent or carer can do is to provide the child or young person with a sense of physical and emotional security and safety. This may seem a relatively straightforward and basic requirement for development, yet, for many of the children and young people we work with, this core condition for development has often been absent.

A sense of safety and security is important for a number of reasons. As the quote above suggests, a sense of being loved and accepted, and having the experience of giving love and having it received, is at the heart of emotional security. The child who is given unconditional love and acceptance feels that 'no matter what mistakes I make or what losses or hurts I experience, I am, at some fundamental and deep level, okay and of worth. I am basically good and lovable. I matter and I can endure. Having this sense of myself makes it easier for me to take care of myself, develop relationships and stand up for myself in life.' This is a key factor in the development of self-worth and resilience.

The belief that we are safe and secure is also important because so much of development is about learning. In order to learn we need to be able explore our environment, try new things and take some risks. If we do not feel there is a place of safety and warmth that we can return to and rely on, it is much harder for us to venture out. Or we may venture out without any thought and be reckless about our own safety or that of others.

Our need for security and safety changes over time. The newborn infant, who is unable to meet any of her own basic needs, requires almost continual physical and emotional reassurance and soothing. The carer who is attentive, warm and responsive gives the baby an experience of physical and emotional security, teaching her that there are people who can be trusted and that the world is mostly an okay place for her to be in. However, if the infant learns to mistrust because her needs go unmet or because responses are inconsistent and unpredictable, she will carry this sense of mistrust forward into the next stages of her development and is likely to suffer from an abiding sense of insecurity. You may need to think about how you 'reattune' to the 'baby' stage of your child. As the book progresses, we will explore in more detail what it means to be an 'attuned' carer (Chapter Three) and how rhythms and routines can be helpful in nurturing a sense of safety (Chapter Five).

What supports toddlers' development is also related to warm, predictable caregiving and a trusted primary caregiver. Toddlers' development is also supported by encouragement to explore the environment and develop their skills with a little more autonomy. Parents who are overly protective or overly permissive may not provide the child with the guidance and support they need to take these first autonomous steps with confidence.

At every stage children need guidance and support to negotiate the world and make the most of the learning opportunities around them. As there are so many things that they don't know about the world, toddlers need a much more hands-on approach to these developmental tasks; attentive and patient caregiving that helps them to understand the limits and boundaries of behaviour will support their development. Encouragement and praise is also very important. Children's need for guidance and support continues throughout childhood and adolescence and works best when it is pitched at their developmental age and capacities. As the book progresses we will give more examples that illustrate the importance of modelling behaviours, reasoning and communicating with children, and helping them to understand and contain their emotions (Chapters Three, Eight, Nine and Ten). Again, your child may have had this stage interrupted or threatened and, despite being chronologically older, will need you to offer some of these 'toddler' experiences.

As children move into later childhood and adolescence and the relationships outside of the home become of increasing importance, it is crucial for parents to support their developing sense of identity. This means helping the child to understand the story of their family and helping them to feel a sense of belonging to the places and people in their life. Later we explore the importance of memories and identity and how you can help children at different stages to develop a coherent and positive narrative about themselves (see Chapter Six). We will also look at how family rituals can help foster a sense of belonging (see Chapter Five).

At every stage it is important to communicate with your child and to model for them what it means to communicate in a caring way. During the earlier years this might involve engaging the child through play of various kinds and helping them to learn words and concepts that will allow them to describe and engage with the world; in the later years of childhood this might involve finding ways to talk about important things in a way that isn't embarrassing or alienating. You may be caring for a child who for reasons of disability or trauma has mastered alternative ways of communicating.

Whatever the age or stage, it is important to listen to your child. Listening requires attending to what is said, what is not said, and what is communicated through behaviour and play. In our work with children we have been continually surprised and delighted by children's capacities for communication, even from a very young age. If we tune in and listen, children have much to tell us and teach us. As the book progresses we will explore more examples of this (see Chapters Three and Nine).

Finally, it is important not to forget how much the external environment and other people impact on the development of the child you are caring for. Opportunities to develop social skills, self-reflective capacities and successes at school are all important in supporting development. Later in the book (Chapter Eleven) we will look in more detail at the importance of social networks and how you as a carer can find ways to maximise the developmental opportunities in the child's wider environment.

Pause for Reflection

What are some of the things you are particularly good at, in terms of supporting your child's development? Are there other ways of supporting development that you would like to become better at? What could help you with this?

Conclusion

In this chapter we have begun to explore how an understanding of human development can help us to be more sensitive and responsive caregivers. We have discussed how it can help us to make sense of behaviour and to understand how children's past experiences impact on them in the present.

We have also begun to explore how attending to developmental needs is so important to helping children recover from past hurts and move on to new experiences. As the book progresses we will explore these needs in more detail and provide lots of examples of how we, and others we have worked with, have used developmental and other theories to help them provide better care to the children and young people they are looking after.

We hope you will read more about child development and human development in the future and we have suggested some further reading that we have found useful.

Further reading and resources

Daniel, B., Wassell, S. and Gilligan, R. (2010) *Child Development for Child Care and Protection Workers*, Second edition. London: Jessica Kingsley Publishers.

Fahlberg, V. (2012) *A Child's Journey through Placement*. London: BAAF.

Gilligan, R. (2001) *Promoting Resilience: A Resource Guide on Working with Children in the Care System*. London: British Agencies for Adoption and Fostering.

Hill, M., Stafford, A., Seaman, P., Ross, N. and Daniel, B. (2007) *Parenting and Resilience*. York: Joseph Rowntree Foundation. Available at: www.jrf.org.uk/sites/files/jrf/parenting-resilience-children.pdf (accessed 29 March 2015).

3

Tuning in and Attunement

Introduction

This chapter is about the process of getting to know a child or young person and developing a relationship of trust and reciprocity. Tuning in is a bit like trying to find a radio station on an analogue radio. This may sound easier than it is. It can be difficult to locate the signal for a station, sometimes the sound comes in and out and there can be lots of interference in the tuning process. Like a radio, each of us has our own unique frequency and if we want to communicate effectively we need to be able to tune into the frequency of others.

Tuning in is about all the things we do to try and understand and communicate with someone else. It requires curiosity, patience, understanding and flexibility. The task of tuning in can be more complex when we are working with children and young people with experiences of loss, neglect and abuse. As we move into a more abiding relationship with a child or young person we move beyond tuning in to attunement. Attunement is about exchange, reciprocity and empathy. It is about really knowing the child and, in turn, the child knowing and trusting you. A recognisable example of attunement are mothers who can tell very quickly, just from the sound of their child's crying, whether the cause of upset is something more minor or something which requires a trip to Accident and Emergency!

Drawing on relevant research and the experiences of carers and social workers, this chapter will examine what tuning in is and why it is important, the skills it requires and how these can be developed. It will seek to answer these key questions:

- How can I understand a child who seems to be emotionally distant or who pushes me away?

- What can I do if I just don't feel like I am clicking with a child?

- What can I do if a child makes me feel uncomfortable?

- How can I give something of myself and still feel I am being 'professional'?

The importance of tuning in and attunement

Pause for Reflection

In order to understand what 'tuning in' is and why it is important, it can be helpful to reflect on some of your own experiences. Think back to your own childhood or adolescence. Was there someone who made a real effort to understand you? What did they do to get to know you? How did it feel to be understood?

Many people say that two of the most important things that a parent, carer or teacher did to understand them was to spend time with them and listen to them. Spending time together was often described as 'quality time' doing things that both the adult and child enjoyed. Many of the carers we have worked with over the years have also spoken about the importance of quality time. They describe this as time when there are few distractions and when they can really focus on developing their connection with their child. At such moments, the adult can focus on the child above all else and, in turn, the child gets to experience being the centre of the universe, the most important person. For many children who are in substitute care settings, this is not an experience they are familiar with.

However, to fully understand tuning in and attunement we have to go back to the start of life. What happens to us when we are babies establishes many of the building blocks for our future relationships. One of the crucial things that attuned parents do for their babies is to respond to their cues and signalling behaviours in a sensitive and timely way. This sensitive, responsive behaviour on the part of the caregiver teaches the baby that relationships are about mutuality and exchange. The baby also learns that relationships are rewarding and, over time, he develops a rich repertoire of cues and responses that helps him to engage in the social world. As he becomes more skilled at this process of engagement, the rewards grow, not only for him but also for those with whom he has relationships.

In order to respond in a sensitive and timely way the parent needs to maintain a focus on the baby. Some new parents talk about becoming totally besotted with their baby and fascinated with each little response and development. This is sometimes described as a 'babymoon' or 'babybubble', a time when new parents are overjoyed with experiencing and getting to know their baby. They may also describe this as a time when they are totally 'loved up'; their hearts are so very full with love for their child.

In fact, love, one of the most profound and ineffable of emotions, is closely linked to the notion of attunement. As Golding and Hughes (2012) explain, 'Love exists in the mutual attunement of two people, each influencing the other.' The developing relationship between baby and parent depends on exchange. Many of a baby's innate behaviours are designed to pull the parent into a process of mutual engagement and discovery. The more responsive the parenting, the more the natural capacities of the baby are developed and enhanced. Both parent and baby find the experience of mutual exchange pleasurable and are changed through the experience. While this is a wonderful experience for many parents, others miss out on this for various reasons and we will talk more about this in a moment.

For babies, showing upset or distress is most often a means of signalling the parent to respond to basic needs such as being fed, having their nappy changed, being cuddled or wanting to play. By responding with curiosity and sensitivity the parents signals to the child that his thoughts and feelings matter and can be understood by others. The parent is also demonstrating an ability to reflect on her own thoughts and feelings and the impact they are having on the child.

Although the parent bears a greater responsibility for the process of tuning in and attunement, attunement is not a one-way process. For love and connectedness to grow there needs to be mutuality and exchange. For this reason, attunement is a process of discovery for all of those involved. Learning about the thoughts, feelings and minds of others is one of the key points of learning for the child. Responding to something another person says or does requires an ability to imagine what they might be feeling or thinking and to anticipate how that person might perceive and react to what you do or say. Some theorists have described this as mentalisation, or the ability to think about thinking. As we also explore in Chapter Five, responsive carers help children to understand their own thoughts and feelings, thus helping them to think about and anticipate what others think and feel as well. As the child develops, his capacity to understand his own feelings and thoughts and those of others will evolve depending on what kind of experiences he has had. Caregivers who are curious about his thoughts and feelings and who wonder with him about what might be generating the feelings that he has will support his development in attunement.

Opportunities for play are also crucial to this process. Through imaginative play children explore and integrate things they are seeing in the social world around them. In pretending to be teacher, parent, baby, they develop and explore the minds of others and try to make sense of the motivations, perspectives and feelings of those around them. In other words, they develop the ability to mentalise.

Thinking about thinking and understanding their own mind and the minds of others is closely linked to the idea of empathy; empathising with a child means trying to understand his inner world and how this inner world influences his experience of the outside world. The capacity to empathise is most likely to develop where children are given experiences of empathy. This is also essential for tuning in and attunement.

Pause for Reflection

Think about a child or young person who is in your care. What do you know about this child's early experiences of parenting? Did the child have some experience of attuned, responsive parenting? How do you think these experiences have influenced how he relates to others now?

For some children with particular disabilities, such as autism, there may be problems in the way their brain processes information, which make it more difficult for them to understand the minds of others. It is important to remember that autism, like many disabilities, is on a spectrum. This means that some individuals may be more able then others to engage in two-way interaction and understand others. Parents and carers need to understand how the impairment impacts on their child and how they see the world. This requires imagination and a willingness to pay close attention to all the available verbal and non-verbal communication the child is providing. Carers may assume that this task is more difficult with disabled children because communication is often non-verbal. However, in our experience, the process of tuning in is similar for all human beings. Whether we have a disability or we don't, human beings have a basic need to communicate. We will use whatever strategies we can to try and do this.

Making sense of these strategies can be more difficult when they are very different to the strategies we might use, but this is why tuning in is so important.

Pause for Reflection

Think about a child you know who may or may not have a disability. Imagine what the world might be like through the eyes of this person. How much can he hear? What can he see? Is he able to gather information through touching things? Is he able to filter out sounds or sights that are non-essential? How long does it take him to process information? What verbal sounds is he able to make? What non-verbal gestures is he able to make? Are there times when he seems to want to communicate more than other times? What might he be trying to tell you or others at these times? How do you feel when you are trying to communicate with him? How do you think he feels about communicating with you?

How to tune in and become attuned

Tuning in is the first step on the road to attunement and requires doing and being in certain ways. Tuning in requires that we do things like listen, respond, engage and spend time with our child. However, simply doing these things will not enable us to deeply connect to our child unless we can do them in a way that conveys warmth, acceptance and curiosity. If we think back to our reflections at the beginning of the chapter, many of us may recognise that in some ways the things that a caring adult did to get to know us were only part of the story. It may seem looking back that the way we felt being around them was significant. Perhaps it seemed that just being with them made us feel good and made us feel special.

Spotlight on Practice

Reflecting with a group of carers, we were struck by the story of Nancy and her two grandmothers. Both of Nancy's grandmothers were interested in her and spent time with her when she was a little girl. Both engaged her in activities and took her on outings and she loved them both very much. However, Nancy spoke about Granny Marie with particular fondness saying, 'It just felt so good to be around her. It was like sitting in a pool of sunshine. I felt so loved whenever I was with her.' There was something about Granny Marie's way of being with Nancy that was about more than what she said and did. How Granny Marie felt about Nancy was almost in the air like an atmosphere that Nancy could feel whenever they were together. This atmosphere also influenced how Nancy responded to Granny Marie, who always got lots of cuddles and appreciation back from Nancy. This exchange between them was a positive feedback loop that served to strengthen, develop and deepen their relationship as the years went by.

Granny Marie and other 'attuned' carers have an abiding, receptive and loving stance towards the child; this creates an atmosphere that the child can feel. However, we would suggest that Granny Marie's ability to convey this feeling to Nancy was not just about her feelings for Nancy. She was also able to know and be tuned into herself. A number of researchers have suggested that in order for us to tune into others we need be tuned into ourselves and have a good relationship with ourselves. Tuning into ourselves means that we are aware of our own feelings and thoughts, and can reflect on our reactions and perceptions. It is important to take time to do this regularly, in whatever way works for us. This could include a regular coffee with a good friend, an afternoon swim or a long bath.

Having a good relationship with ourselves also means that we have mostly positive thoughts about ourselves and that we try to be understanding, rather than overly critical, when we get something wrong. When we recognise that no one is perfect, we can be confident enough in ourselves to take on board feedback from others and consider the views of others. It is important to acknowledge to children when we get something wrong or we have missed out on something they were trying to tell us. For example, if you are having a difficult day where you are finding it hard to connect to the child, it can be helpful to say something like, 'Things feel a bit jaggy today. I feel like I have been missing you today and I am sorry. I wonder why that might be?' In sharing your awareness with the child you are showing them how to tune in, even when this is difficult. You are also showing them that these things can be understood and connections re-established.

The capacity to tune in is also heavily influenced by the environment we are living in and the number of physical and emotional demands placed on us. If we are pre-occupied with worries or we are physically and emotionally exhausted because we have not had the time to look after ourselves, it will be very hard for us to be available and receptive to others. Many of the children we work with have lived in environments that do not support tuned in parenting. Many of their parents were living on very limited incomes and found it a struggle to ensure basic needs were met. Housing may have been overcrowded and of poor quality. Relationships between parents may have been violent or antagonistic. For children whose parents engaged in problematic drug or alcohol use, their experiences of attunement were likely very limited and, in turn, affected their own capacity to tune into others.

Pause for Reflection

Are there things in your environment that are getting in the way of your ability to tune into yourself or others? Which of these things do you think you might be able to do something about? Would attending to your own self-care affect them? Who could help you with this?

It is important when we are feeling overwhelmed and distracted, that we try to find a moment to ground ourselves. Remember the child will be trying to tune into you, even if his ability to do this is compromised by his previous experiences. He will pick up on your stress and distraction and may react to this in unhelpful ways. Indeed, your feelings of distraction or of being overwhelmed might mirror a much more sustained lack of attunement that he has experienced and may, therefore, be very frightening. If you can tune into yourself and be calm and focused, it will be easier for you to tune into the child and vice versa.

Sometimes it may be hard to know if your efforts to tune into a child are working. It is important to reflect on your efforts and the child's reactions and ask the question: Am I tuned into this child? How would I know if I were? Your own thoughts and feelings are a clue to how the child may be feeling. If you are feeling disconnected or out of touch, angry or alienated, then chances are that the child is too. It can be helpful to reflect on this with the child.

Spotlight on Practice

Bill was a 15-year-old boy who was regularly described by agencies as 'difficult to engage'. He did not attend appointments, he rarely attended school and his time in the residential unit was limited to sleeping there and an occasional meal. He didn't 'cause trouble' when he was around but he avoided staff. He rarely said much and any responses to questions were brief and limited on detail. This young man had experienced multiple losses in his life and viewed connections to others as a risk; with connection came the possibility of loss.

Over time, Margo, a night shift worker, was able to develop a connection with Bill. She would chat to him gently while making him his evening snack (which he never asked for when he returned home late to the unit but always ate enthusiastically). Over months she learned a few things about his interests and habits; she learned that he would take long walks all over the city, often returning to neighbourhoods where he had lived with his mum years ago. In time she found out about his dream to have a flat in a particular area of the city and she slowly began to help him with the steps involved in making this a reality. Margo was a very gentle, quiet person, but she knew how to convey to the young people that she was interested in them. She was patient and willing to wait and develop the relationship at a pace Bill felt comfortable with. Margo was just the kind of person he liked; she didn't expect too much of him and she was not loud or forceful. His quietness didn't bother

her and she was happy to potter about the kitchen quietly while he ate his snack. In tuning into Bill, Margo followed Bill's cues. She did not get annoyed or impatient at his perceived lack of engagement; she continued to reach out with gentle care. She respected the fact that Bill's behaviour was his shield against being hurt again, and she did not try to take this from him.

Tuning in is delicate work. Each child or young person has a different set of experiences and needs, and it may take a long time for you to find a way to reach him. Sometimes you may find it impossible to tune into a particular child or young person. This may have to do with subtle incompatibilities between you and the child that are at the level of unconscious feelings. Autumn remembers working with a young woman who took a strong and immediate dislike to her that was never overcome. The reasons for this were unclear but it was probably the case that Autumn reminded her of someone associated with pain and loss. This felt like a failure and the rejection was painful, but it is important to recognise that sometimes there is just no way to find that fit or connection, and in such cases it may be helpful to explore whether there are other adults who can do some of this important tuning in work until the child feels more confident and trusting.

What you may notice

Many of the children we have worked with have missed out on a caring, responsive parent who delights in them and is able to focus on them in a consistent way. As a result, many of these children have developed unhelpful strategies to get the attention of adults. These strategies may include anger and aggression, or withdrawn, avoidant behaviours. They may also move back and forth between these two strategies in a way that is confusing for caregivers.

Many children, and particularly those with disabilities such as autism, are very sensitive to the sensory environment. They can struggle to filter and order sensory information, and find crowds, noise and new environments incredibly confusing and anxiety provoking. They many engage in repetitive or ritualistic behaviours as a way to try to calm themselves or to communicate their stress to caregivers.

Children you care for may also have limited experience of a positive reciprocal relationship with a primary caregiver. As a result, they struggle to interpret the behaviour or understand the minds of others. They may have a limited repertoire for social engagement. Their attempts to engage others may suggest they are not picking up on the social cues that might help them to understand what others are thinking or feeling. This may be because they struggle to mentalise, having not had the opportunities to develop these skills or the experience of being held in mind and attuned to by others.

Spotlight on Practice

Jenny was 14 when she was placed in residential care for the first time. She had been living in a physically and emotionally abusive situation her whole life. She had also been sexually abused by one of her mother's former boyfriends. Jenny had missed a lot of her education but she loved to read; her teachers said she had a natural aptitude for learning and was very bright. However, Jenny struggled to make friends and seemed to annoy all of the other children in the residential unit where she lived. Many of the staff commented on the fact that they found her annoying and her behaviour was often described as 'attention seeking'.

Jenny's lack of an experience of attuned parenting meant that she found it difficult to read social situations. When other young people were in a quiet mood and happily engaged with some activity, Jenny would bound up to them and poke them or try to get them up to do something else that she wanted to do. Because she found it difficult to read what others wanted or felt, she struggled to judge how to approach them.

Jenny would often follow staff around the residential unit talking incessantly and asking them personal or inappropriate questions. When staff showed an interest in her and tried to tune into her, she would often respond with intense enthusiasm at first. She would want this person's constant attention and would find it hard to share them with other staff or children. Attempts by staff to set some boundaries with her were often perceived as a rejection and she would become very withdrawn and upset, saying terrible things to the person to get back at them for their perceived rejection.

Jenny's inner world was swirling with lots of complex and difficult emotions. At an unconscious level she was desperate for others to help her manage and regulate all these emotions. However, because she had not learned how to participate in a caring relationship involving mutuality and exchange, her attempts to draw in others inevitably backfired. This would leave her feeling worse than ever.

Although not all children will show their feelings as powerfully as Jenny, we can all think of children we have cared for who were hard to connect with for one reason or another. For engagement to be successful we need to be able to tune in. To do so, we really need to try and understand the inner world of the child as well as his likes and dislikes, his hopes, dreams and fears. If it is hard to tune into a child then this probably tells us something important about his previous experiences of care and whether or not he has ever experienced attunement from a carer or parent.

Children who have missed out on attuned parenting tend to adopt extreme behaviours of one kind or another. Like the terrified baby who either screams uncontrollably or plays dead to try and get their needs met or to avoid abusive responses, these children have not had the opportunities to learn about the joys and pleasure of a caring exchange. Extreme behaviours may have been crucial to their survival in another environment, but are no longer needed in a safe, more caring environment. However, survival behaviours learned over a long time take time to unlearn. It may be frustrating for carers to see these behaviours continue when there seems to be no 'need' for them anymore (see Chapter Ten for further discussion about these kind of behaviours and how they might be understood and managed).

It is also worth remembering that children with disabilities are far more likely to have been abused or neglected then other children. There are many reasons for this including opportunity – abusers know it is harder for a disabled child to communicate to someone that they are being abused. Although a disabled child will be dealing with all the fear and terror that any abused child experiences, it may be far more difficult for them to express and make sense of these feelings. It is important for carers not to assume that the behaviours of a disabled child simply relate to a communication impairment; they may in fact be the child expressing distress and trauma that has gone unrecognised.

Where there has been an absence of attuned parenting the capacity for empathy may also be underdeveloped. Some carers have spoken to us in great distress about children who don't seem to care about the feelings of others and even show cruelty to animals or other children. Abuse involves a misuse of power, and those who have experienced abuse of various types often talk about how frightening it is to feel powerless. There will be a lot of different feelings and unconscious processes going on inside a child who seems not to care about hurting others or even seems to enjoy it. Chronic abuse and neglect are the opposite of attuned parenting and children with this experience may have learned that relationships are about being dominated or dominating, being controlled or being controlling. For them, dominating exchanges may feel like a way of connecting to others and this might be one of the ways they have learned to engage in relationships.

Carers may find it particularly difficult when a child has hurt them or someone else and just doesn't seem to care. This lack of empathy for you or others may be very frightening and may make you angry. This is understandable and we will talk more in Chapter Ten about dealing with aggression. It is useful to remember, however, that the foundations for our empathic capacities are laid down in experiences of attunement and security in early childhood. If a child has missed out on these experiences it will take time to offer the experiences that will help to repair and develop their innate capacities for empathy. It can be helpful to remember that human beings have an immense and inborn capacity for the development of empathy. Researchers from a range of disciplines including evolutionary biology, neuroscience and psychology are exploring how our immense capacities for empathy are, in part, a function of how our brain has evolved, and that these capacities are part of the success story of the human species. In the final section of this chapter we will provide some more suggestions for how you might support the child you are working with to develop their empathic capacities.

What you may feel

Tuning in requires paying attention to the feelings that the child or young person is evoking in us. Feelings are often held in the body. If you're not sure, notice your body the next time you are feeling very stressed. Your shoulders will be tense, your breath may be more shallow, your palms may be sweaty and your stomach queasy. These are examples of emotions acting on the body. Paying attention to how you feel in your body and mind when you are around the child, or have just been with them, can help you understand and tune into how they are feeling. Do you feel anxious and tense? Angry and wound up? Unsettled and uncomfortable in your own skin? If the child is evoking these feelings in you there is a good chance that this is how the child is feeling on the inside. Your thoughts and feelings are clues to understanding the child. This means you need to pay attention to them and acknowledge them, even if you may feel guilty about the feelings you are having (as the example of Jenny illustrates).

As we discussed earlier in the chapter, when development is going well and an attuned relationship begins to grow, there are huge rewards for the parent as well as the child. So what you feel may also be very positive. A child who enjoys your company and responds to your attempts at engagement with smiles and laughter is hugely affirming. As a carer you feel that you are doing a good job. You feel satisfaction in knowing that your child is developing and learning about how to cooperate with others and enjoy their company. You feel their love and care for you, which is nourishing and helps sustain you through more challenging episodes of behaviour.

It can be more difficult to sustain your efforts at tuning in if you feel you are getting very little back from the child. Leslie Ironside has written about the emotional cost of working with traumatised and abused children and young people and we have included the details of an article she has written in the 'Further reading and resources' section at the end of this chapter (Ironside 2004). She explains that children who have had traumatic backgrounds may not know themselves very well and, as a result, may find it difficult to let others know them. The process of tuning in, and the eventual attunement that flows from a sustained and successful process of tuning in, can be blocked both consciously and unconsciously by the child. With a sense of self that feels fractured and frayed it is hard to share or let others in. The child may fear what others will see if he lets them come closer. His feelings may include shame and guilt for things he doesn't understand or believes were his fault. He may have also been told that he is bad or evil by previous caregivers and may worry that this is true.

Spotlight on Practice

Returning to Jenny, staff found it hard to work with her and many said she made them feel uncomfortable. Jenny's long-standing unmet need for a nurturing experience of dependency meant that she came across as incredibly demanding, attention seeking and needy. Some staff responded to this by working harder to keep her at a distance. However, this only resulted in Jenny's behaviours becoming more and more extreme, culminating in a number of attempts to take her own life.

Given the intensity and extremity of Jenny's emotional life, it is not surprising that many staff found her difficult to work with. Working with Jenny could be overwhelming and frightening. In the face of so much unmet need staff could sometimes feel as hopeless as Jenny.

It was also hard to admit that at times Jenny was not an easy child to like. Her attempts to engage with others were so unskilled that it could be very frustrating and emotionally taxing to spend time with her. The guilt associated with having these feelings towards Jenny made it even harder to work with her; staff felt like they were failing in their work.

When the staff team began to acknowledge and work with the strong feelings that Jenny provoked, they began to understand her better.

They became less reactive and more compassionate in their responses to her. Some of them found time and space to talk to Jenny about their struggle to connect with her and what this might be about. With time Jenny began to develop new skills in talking about her own feelings and managing them.

It is really important to acknowledge just how challenging it can be to tune into children who have been traumatised, abused and neglected. These children can evoke strong emotions in the people who work with them and care for them. The glimpses they give us into their inner world can evoke fear, revulsion, anger and despair. It is important to talk about these feelings with someone we trust in order to make sense of them, learn from them and avoid becoming overwhelmed by them. These feelings also offer important clues about the inner world of the child – if we deny or ignore them out of shame or fear we will miss out on the chance to better understand the child and ourselves.

Despite how challenging it can be to tune into some children, we have also found that the rewards of connecting and engaging with children are immense. Autumn recalls working with a young man of 15 who, after several care placements and a stay in a secure unit, was finally able to connect with some of the workers who had been trying to engage with him for over a year. In one meeting not long after moving back into a more open residential setting he acknowledged just how much he had tried to push people away and said 'thanks for not giving up on me'. For the group of professionals involved this was a wonderful and satisfying moment.

How you and others can help

Spending quality time with the child or young person is a key step in the process of tuning in and attunement. This should be time when you can really focus on the child above all else. Listen carefully to what the child is saying to you through his *behaviours*, as well as with his words. Show an interest in what interests him and look out for opportunities to develop and nurture these interests through shared activities. Autumn remembers working with a girl, Lori, who defined herself as a 'goth'. There were many afternoons visiting 'goth' shops, listening to bands like Marilyn Manson in the car. This was not something Autumn would have chosen to do on her own and she even acknowledged to Lori that this was not really her thing, but she explained she wanted to experience it with Lori because it was so important to her. In our experience, children and young people appreciate these efforts immensely.

Sharing a common rhythm can help to bring people together and facilitate tuning in and attunement. So, for example, dancing together, singing together, playing catch or even walking together at a similar pace all give children a direct and immediate experience of reciprocity, engagement and connectedness, and they are also fun. Having fun and sharing a laugh also help to build a sense of connection: we understand each other enough to be able to laugh about the same thing. In Chapter Five we will explore in detail the importance of rhythm and routine for children.

Don't be afraid to wonder *with* the child about things. In this way you will model the skill of thinking about thinking and you also help the child make sense of his behaviours and feelings. Being curious about the child and about yourself will help you to tune in. Check in with yourself regularly and ask am I tuning in right now? If you feel distracted or caught up with intense feelings try to notice them, put them to one side for examination later and re-focus on being a calm, loving presence for the child.

It is also important to help children to name their feelings by supporting them to develop their emotional vocabulary. There are a range of useful games and activities for doing this (see the 'Further reading and resources' section at the end), but don't forget they can learn by your example. Be willing to talk about your own feelings. However, you should also make sure you have a safe adult place to work through your feelings and get support. Your relationship to yourself is so important to your ability to tune into a child or young person. Don't neglect it.

Try to cultivate a hopeful and loving stance in relation to the child. Many children will be able to feel this. In fact, remember that the child will be trying to understand you, if only to protect himself from what he perceives as an unknown threat. His previous experiences may limit his capacities to 'read' and understand the minds of others but he will still be trying to feel his way into a new situation, full of strangers. He will be studying your habits, body language and tone of voice. Try to find ways to help him to get to know you. Remember, attunement is not a one-way process. If he is going to feel safe with you, he needs to know you. This does not mean that nothing can be private; it is neither safe nor helpful to lack boundaries around what is personal to you. However, there is much you can share about yourself, your likes and dislikes and some of your experiences, without risk of overloading the child or exposing yourself too much. Consider how you would feel living with a bunch of strangers. You would want to know something about them to begin to feel comfortable and safe.

It is also important to remember that some children will actively evade our efforts to tune into them. This may be a very important survival strategy that they developed when they lived in an unsafe environment and they may have very good reasons to distrust all adults. It would be inappropriate to expect the child to abandon these behaviours overnight. It will take time for him to feel safe in his new home. Once this sense of safety begins to emerge he may be able to test out some new strategies for engaging with others, but every child will move at their own pace. It is important to be understanding and gentle with him and with yourself and to find ways to sustain your hope and enthusiasm when the child is giving you very little back.

Tuning into a child who has disabilities, particularly when these are complex and include learning and communication difficulties, may be very challenging for carers. So much of our world is dominated by verbal communication, we may struggle to adapt our approach to the needs of the child. All carers need to experiment with ways of reaching the child in their care; however, carers of children with disabilities may need to think more deeply about this and experiment with tools that can enhance non-verbal communication. **Talking Mats** and strategies such as **Intensive Interaction** are being used with great success by some carers and we would encourage you to explore such approaches. Further information about these is offered at the end of the chapter.

Not giving up is key to the tuning in and attunement process, but sometimes we need to acknowledge that we or the service we provide cannot meet the needs of the child at this time. That doesn't mean we are giving up on him. We have worked with many carers who have maintained links with children and young people who were placed with them for many years after they have moved on to other placements or independent living. These carers have been a point of connection and continuity for children and young people even when they no longer lived with them. They were able to tune into the children and young people they worked with and this enabled an abiding connection to develop, which remained important to both parties long after the placement ended. For example, Sylvia, a residential worker, talked about a visit from a young woman who she had worked with. The girl had said to Sylvia, 'I always knew you cared and that helped when I didn't care about myself.' Efforts to tune into the child convey an important message to him about his fundamental worth, even when the relationship does not always deepen into the kind of abiding attunement that we have talked about earlier.

Everyday things you might like to try

Now that you have reflected on the meaning of tuning in and attunement, you might want to get started right away with trying something new. The suggestions below could be a good place to start. However, we hope that you will remember to reflect on these strategies in the light of the theory we have just discussed in this chapter. Notice how you are feeling and what you are thinking as you undertake these activities. How do you think the child is feeling? Do you feel more connected as a result? How do you know this is the case? We also hope you will try to make these everyday opportunities; we have found that children respond better when the things we do with them feel natural and are part of the normal flow of day-to-day life.

Tuning into yourself

If you are not tuned into yourself it will be very hard to tune into others. For this reason we suggest that you begin by trying new ways of tuning into yourself. The body can provide important cues for us about how we are feeling. More and more people are using **mindfulness** techniques like meditation or quiet reflection time to help them tune into their own bodies and their feelings. If you have had a busy, jumbled day where you feel it has been hard to connect to yourself or others it can be helpful to find a quiet place to sit for 5 minutes. It may be that you can begin to do aspects of this exercise with your child or encourage your child to try it on his own. Let's try it now. Just follow these steps:

1. Find a quiet comfortable place to sit where you will not be disturbed for the next 5 minutes. Make sure your back is straight and your hands and feet are uncrossed. Close your eyes.

2. Take ten slow steady deep breaths in and out.

3. As you breathe in notice the breath filling your lungs and imagine that it is moving outward to fill the rest of your body.

4. As you exhale imagine the breath taking the stress and weariness of the day away with it.

5. Continue to breathe slowly and steadily in and out.

6. Turn your focus to your body and notice any points of tension. Breathe into these places and imagine the fatigue and tension drifting away.

7. How do you feel now? How does your body feel? What's your emotional state like? Do you feel more or less receptive to others?

Tuning into the child

- Make the most of opportunities to *share space and time with the child*. This might be organised activities but it could also be just sitting in the room with him while he does something on his own. Pay attention to what the child is doing and saying while he is playing, and respond to any openings from him to engage in discussion. You may want to use some of the reflection techniques discussed in Chapter Nine.

• Take the time to *get to know what the child likes and dislikes* and what their interests are. *Let him teach you* about a topic or interest and try to understand why it is important to him. *Consider developing one of these interests into a bigger shared project.* For example, help him to decorate his room with pictures and colours relating to his favourite football team or band. As you do this with the child, remember to reflect on your own feelings. What do you feel about their likes or dislikes? How might these feelings be impacting on your relationship?

• *Spend time playing a game that requires mutuality and exchange* (e.g. catch, patty cake, hide and seek, snap). Getting into a physical rhythm of engagement with a child can be a first step in a process of tuning in (see Chapter Five for more ideas about using rhythms, routines and rituals to develop and enhance relationships). Notice how you are feeling when playing the game with the child. What do you think the child is feeling? How is he communicating this?

• *Name your emotions and help children to develop their emotional vocabulary.* You can make this fun by using *games and worksheets* (see for example the *Big Book of Blob Feelings* listed at the end of this chapter; Wilson and Long 2008). For older children and adolescents, try watching *films* and *reading* age-appropriate books together. Choose films that help young people think about the emotional worlds and experiences of others and use them as a way of *getting conversations started about interpreting emotions.* We have listed a few examples of films and books we have used for this purpose at the end of the chapter. Some of them are very emotive and include adult content so be sure to review them first to make sure they are suitable for the age and stage of the child.

- *Looking out for opportunities for role play (this could include puppets or toys)* can also be an excellent way to provide learning about emotions and how to be caring. Many children enjoy playing mother or father with baby dolls or playing doctor and nursing sick toys or animals. Engaging children in these games can help you understand what they have learned about caring for others or what they are trying to make sense of about this. Playing with them can also give you another opportunity to model empathy and care. We have found that children and even adolescents often love engaging with puppets and will have some very interesting conversations when they are talking to a puppet or playing at being one.

Conclusion

Human beings are social creatures. From the moment of our birth we are seeking out connection with others. This is one of our strengths and the source of our greatest vulnerability. If those who care for us cannot tune into us and respond to our attempts to engage them, we may not learn all of the important lessons about social engagement and exchange. Without another person to provide us with feedback and guidance we may not learn how to differentiate and manage the many emotional states we experience. We may not get the opportunity to experience ourselves as a person, who is full of goodness, can bring joy to others and who has a unique perspective on the world to share.

The good news is that it seems that even those of us who have been hurt very badly still crave connection with others. In our experience it is possible to reach the child if we are willing to tune in and we are persistent. Many children and young people have been able to move on from incredibly abusive and neglectful experiences to positive and rewarding relationships with themselves and others. You can be part of this hopeful future for the child. This can be difficult and exhausting work, but when we have moments of attunement with the child the rewards for both of us are immense. This makes the job worth doing.

Further reading and resources

Cairns, K. (2002) *Attachment, Trauma and Resilience: Therapeutic Caring for Children.* London: BAAF.

Gerhardt, S. (2004) *Why Love Matters: How Affection Shapes a Baby's Brain.* Hove: Brunner-Routledge.

Ironside, L. (2004) 'Living a provisional existence: Thinking about foster carers and the emotional containment of children placed in their care.' *Adoption and Fostering 28*, 4, 39–49.

Rae, T. (2007) *Dealing with Feelings.* London: Sage.

Wilson, P. and Long, I. (2008) *The Big Book of Blob Feelings.* London: Speechmark Publishing Ltd.

For a short film about brain development and relationships, with Dr Suzanne Zeedyk, go to:

www.educationscotland.gov.uk/learningandteaching/earlylearningandchildcare /prebirthtothree/nationalguidance/conversations/suzannezeedyk.asp

For more information about Intensive Support for people with severe learning disabilities or autism go to:

www.intensiveinteraction.co.uk

For more information about the communication tool Talking Mats go to:

www.talkingmats.com

Books for children and young people

Green, J. (2012) *The Fault in Our Stars.* London: Penguin.

Lowry, L. (2008) *The Giver.* London: HarperCollins.

McCloud, C. (2006) *Have You Filled a Bucket Today? A Guide to Daily Happiness for Kids.* Northville, MI: Nelson Publishing and Marketing.

Salinger, J.D. (1951) *The Catcher in the Rye.* London: Penguin.

Spinelli, J. (2002) *Stargirl.* London: Orchard Books.

Films for older young people

Gimme Shelter (2013)

Pay it Forward (2000)

Sweet Sixteen (2002)

4

Healing and Containing
Relationships as a Source of Recovery

Introduction

This chapter explores ways to create healing and containing homes that will support a child in learning to manage experiences and emotions. As discussed in Chapter Two, part of a child's social, emotional and cognitive development involves learning to use thinking in order to manage emotions. Trauma, abuse and neglect, however, can get in the way of this, and therefore as carers we may have to provide children with opportunities to achieve this crucial development.

The word 'containment' is sometimes used negatively in relation to child care – usually to describe keeping a lid on things or being overly controlling. This is definitely *not* what is meant here by containment. Quite the opposite, a carer who has a containing effect (in the way we are using the term here) brings about a feeling of relief and an increased sense of capability to those around her. A containing relationship or environment enables people to feel safe, understood, respected and positively challenged. It is not too tight or constraining, and it is not too loose or overly indulgent. A containing environment includes more than just the physical environment, though the physical environment is an important part. It is also made up of the rhythms, routines, expectations and predictable responses that go on in a home (these will be discussed further in Chapters Five and Ten). Most important, though, are the relationships within a containing space.

The chapter starts with discussing what is meant by the term 'containment' before moving on to describe what happens when there is a lack of containment. A discussion of how containment works and what carers need to be able to provide containment for children will follow. Finally, it will end with some suggestions about how containment can be provided for children in your care.

The chapter will address questions commonly encountered by carers, including:

- What can I do for a child who seems to blow up all the time?

- How do I deal with the way a child makes me feel?

- What kinds of things might I suggest to my employing organisation to support me in caring for a child?

Containing environments and containment

The word **containment** refers to the processes that help a person to become able to use thinking to manage their experiences and emotions; it comes from the work of Wilfred Bion (1962). Building on the work of Bion and others, Hazel Douglas offers an excellent definition of containment:

> *Containment is thought to occur when one person receives and understands the emotional communication of another without being overwhelmed by it, processes it and then communicates understanding and recognition back to the other person. This process can restore capacity to think in the other person.*
>
> *(Douglas 2007, p.33)*

Typically, the initial processes of containment happen naturally during the first few years of life. Containment and attachment (as discussed in Chapter Two) are closely related, and a child's primary attachment figure usually provides his first experiences of containment. When an infant experiences unbearable pain, discomfort, fear or confusion, someone (usually a parent) is tuned into what is wrong and provides relief. That person contains the unmanageable and makes it manageable. This can be in the form of a changed nappy, a filled belly or all of the numerous other activities that parents and carers do for infants throughout each day. These activities are frequently accompanied by active soothing and by the verbal identification of emotions and experiences. It is through these processes that children begin to learn how to use thinking to manage experiences and emotions. For children with severe learning disabilities, the development of thinking to manage experiences and emotions may be affected; they may remain more dependent on containing environments and relationships.

It is useful to pause and remember that when we are first born, we have no ability to distinguish ourselves from the world around us and no way of making sense of our own emotions and experiences. Everything is just raw experience that we are unable to understand. The ability to think about things rather than simply feel and react comes about from our early experiences of containment. It is fundamental to our development. It is also easy to take this ability for granted; it can be such a natural part of everything we do that it is not something we actually remember learning.

This process of being able to manage experiences and emotions develops gradually, thus our instinctive expectations of a 3-year-old in relation to containment will not be the same as for a 10-year-old. For example, the ability to cope with the disappointment of a denied request for a highly desired item in the supermarket will typically be more difficult for a 3-year-old, and his emotions may come spilling out in the form of tears or tantrums. A 10-year-old who has had a good foundation in the development of containment will be less likely to find that disappointment unmanageable under the same circumstances, but he still might have a hard time accepting 'no', especially if he is tired, stressed or also having to manage other difficult feelings or experiences. This example also highlights the fluid nature of containment – it isn't something that a child simply achieves on his journey of development. Rather, it is something he is more or less able to do depending on his early experiences of care, his relative level of development, any cognitive impairment he might have and the degree of challenging circumstances he finds himself having to manage.

A lack of containment: What you might notice

Some of the children you care for may have had disruptions to these early experiences of containment and therefore are less able to use thinking to manage their experiences and emotions. The impact of this can affect their learning and social development; more concretely, it can make events throughout the day unmanageable and even painful. A child with uncontained feelings is pretty easy to recognise. We might refer to him as 'going to pieces' or 'coming apart at the seams', and our natural instinct is to try and help hold him together. This can be challenging, however, as the right amount of containment for one child may be too much or too little for another. Providing containment might feel like trying to hold onto a typhoon with one child. With another, it might feel like trying to catch a feather.

Children who regularly experience uncontained emotions can be highly reactive, can struggle to manage transitions like waking up in the morning or going to bed at night, and can have trouble reflecting on their own behaviour and its impact on other people. When they become upset, which may be often, they can have great difficulty responding to your attempts to support them or to set boundaries around their behaviour. Sometimes they can even lose their ability to understand verbal forms of communication.

Spotlight on Practice

Kevin's birthday was last Tuesday and the care team at the residential school decided to surprise him. Dave managed to get the local bakery to make a red velvet cake (Kevin's favourite) with icing to make it look like a football. The team also got him a new football and a computer game he had been talking about all week. When Kevin came in from classes that afternoon, they had the kitchen decorated in red – Kevin's favourite colour. Kevin took one look at everything and blew up. He shouted that he didn't want their 'shitty' cake or presents, and he stormed out, knocking over a chair, shoving the cake onto the floor and tearing one of the streamers from the ceiling.

This encounter was clearly difficult for everyone concerned. It may reflect some of the experiences you have had with your child when you created what you hoped was a positive experience, but it ended up making everyone feel bad. From a containment perspective, we can begin to wonder what is happening for Kevin in this situation that is unmanageable for him. We will return to this question further along in the chapter.

A lack of containment: How you might feel

It is not just children in your care who will have uncontained feelings and experiences sometimes. We all can have feelings and experiences that are so overwhelming that we find it difficult to use thinking to manage them. Most of us can remember feeling so upset that we could not think straight or being in such difficulty that we felt we were 'falling apart'.

Providing care for someone who is regularly uncontained will have an effect on your own level of containment – your own ability to think clearly and manage your emotions. You might notice that you become less reflective and more reactive. This can happen in different ways, from hostile or punitive reactions at one extreme, to a shutting down of emotion and response at the other. The way your face and body convey your feelings may become wooden or flat. Characteristic underlying feelings that are often associated with an uncontained state include overwhelm, confusion or fatigue – along with the emotions that trigger this state to begin with, like fear, anger, hurt or sadness. So both the child and the adult caring for him can end up with these feelings.

Pause for Reflection

Is a lack of containment, or a lack of ability to use thinking to manage feelings and experiences, recognisable in any of the children you care for? What usually happens to let you know that that child is becoming uncontained? How do you feel when this happens?

Sometimes uncontained emotions are less obvious, and individuals or even groups of individuals can be unaware of the disruption to their clear thinking that is taking place. We can look at how our society has become avoidant of risk, especially of risks to children, as an illustrative example. Our anxieties about something bad happening to children, particularly children who are in alternative care, are sometimes so uncontained that we are expected to take disproportionate precautions or avoid doing beneficial activities. One way this is happening can be seen in the increasing rules about touch that are springing up in some organisations, sometimes causing more problems than good. We discuss the use of touch in more depth in Chapter Eight.

It may be useful to step back here and clarify that it is not the desire to avoid bad things happening to children that is the problem. The problem comes when the related fears and anxieties are not contained; that is to say they are not thought about or mentally processed enough and therefore they disable individuals and groups from thinking clearly.

Saying a feeling or experience is contained doesn't mean that all related discomfort disappears; it means that the feelings or experience are processed enough so that the difficult parts are still manageable and do not overwhelm. It means creating space to make sense of what we're feeling and experiencing. For example, sometimes just being able to acknowledge that something scares us or that we feel really angry about something can reduce its power over us, and we can think a bit more clearly about it.

A shift from perceiving unpleasant feelings as a problem to a source of potential information, as well as a natural part of healthy development can make a big difference in your ability to provide containment.

This shift can improve your tolerance of unpleasant, difficult and troubling feelings. In turn, your ability to sit with feelings and think about them improves. You may find that as a result, something seems to change in a positive way without you necessarily having reached a conscious understanding. Given the space provided by your thoughtfulness and lack of interference, you may find that sometimes the child is able to work something out 'on his own'.

Spotlight on Practice

After Kevin stormed out, the care team looked at each other in shock. They had gone to some trouble to make the day special for him, and he had thrown it back in their faces. How could he be so ungrateful? They would never have got away with such behaviour when they were young.

   After only a couple of exchanged comments with team members saying very briefly how they felt, they were able to shift their focus away from their initial feelings of indignation to what might be going on for Kevin to have reacted this way. Sheila, one of the care team, remembered that Kevin had been worried about his Gran lately. Dave, who is probably the most attuned to Kevin, suggested that it may be more than just Kevin's concern about his Gran. Given Kevin's history, he suggested that Kevin may feel he doesn't deserve good things or that they will be snatched from him. Kevin's reaction may have been an attempt to protect himself from those difficult feelings. Being aware of his own initial feelings of 'that ungrateful, undeserving little so-and-so' helped Dave to think about this possibility.

Part of the reason why our own emotions can become more uncontained when working with children whose experiences and emotions are often uncontained has to do with **absorption**. It is one of the mechanisms of containment (or how containment works), and an understanding of these mechanisms can help you maximise the containing potential of your everyday practice in caring for children. We discuss these mechanisms next.

Mechanisms of containment:
How containment works

Absorption or 'soaking it all up!'

The notion of absorption is very similar to attunement (as discussed in Chapter Three). To provide a response that enables thinking and makes the child's feelings and experiences more manageable (in other words, a containing response), you need to have some sense of what is wrong. One of the ways we gain this sense comes from what is referred to as absorption. Indeed, reference is often made to carers *absorbing* the uncontainable, unbearable, unmanageable from the child and giving it back in a more contained, bearable and manageable form.

So what, exactly, is being absorbed? Advances in neurobiology are helping us to see that thoughts and emotions give off electromagnetic signals that affect the chemistry and electricity in every cell of our bodies. We also send out a variety of electrical signals, or vibrations, based on what we are thinking, and some of this is absorbed by others.

Bruce Perry, a neurobiologist who has worked with traumatised children in alternative care settings, describes the physical dimension of absorption:

> *A central aspect of [your neural] network is the capacity to read and respond to the emotional and social cues that are being projected by people you interact with. If they are distracted and distressed, you will feel dismissed; you essentially will feel the way they feel – distressed… We have the neurobiological capacity to absorb and be influenced by the emotions of those around us. (Perry 2009, n.p.)*

We are wired this way so that we can have relationships with one another. Relationships are necessary for our survival. The desire to be understood is innate and deeply instinctive. As newly born infants, we needed our carers to understand what we were feeling – hungry, tired, frightened, wet – so that they could meet our needs. On a very primitive level, we were getting others to feel something as a result of what we were feeling. Often and throughout life, we get people to feel what we are feeling. Sometimes this is conscious and deliberate, but most of the time it is an unconscious process. When it happens unconsciously because the feeling is too uncomfortable to feel on a conscious level, this is called **projection**.

Pause for Reflection

Can you identify some of the ways your child gets you to feel what he is feeling? What does he do verbally, and what does he do non-verbally? Which feelings do you seem to absorb most?

It is helpful, then, to think of absorption as **received communication**. What is being communicated by the child through projection and absorbed by you are the child's feelings, thoughts and experiences that are unmanageable, unbearable and uncontainable. Much of the time they are so intolerable that it is not possible for the child to allow them into his conscious awareness. So in essence, we are sometimes feeling what a child (or even another adult) simply cannot bear to feel even though, paradoxically, the feeling is still present in his subconscious. Also, we are sometimes the ones projecting our own unmanageable, unbearable and uncontainable feelings onto others.

One of the important benefits of knowing about absorption is that it can enhance our understanding of the children we care for. Sometimes there is a disconnection between the emotions that a child presents in his surface behaviour and what is really going on at a deeper level; this is especially the case when the deeper emotions are unbearable, intolerable or uncontainable. For example, a child who presents hostility or even rage may provoke a feeling of fear in you. At one level, the fear may be your own reaction to a threatening situation, but it is also highly possible that you are absorbing the fear or even terror that is uncontainable for the child.

The feelings you may absorb from children might include fear, helplessness, hopelessness, despair, rage, jealousy, overwhelm, betrayal, worthlessness, loss, loneliness or even sexual feelings. Our job is not to take these feelings away, much as we might feel tempted to, but to help children learn to recognise, think about and manage them. Children can have trouble processing positive emotions as well. They can become overwhelmed with euphoria, excitement or idealised feelings about you, which can then be absorbed by you. This is the case for all children and young people (and even, sometimes, adults); it simply may be more complex and intense with children who have had significant disruptions to their early experiences of containment. For example, an event like a birthday party may elicit an over-excited reaction in a child who, without help to contain it, may struggle to manage himself. You may well remember events that you've organised for children that have started well, with everyone being caught up in the good feelings, but have then ended in tears, and this can often be the reason.

We can sometimes become overwhelmed by the powerful emotions we absorb. It is also very challenging to manage our own feelings triggered by what we absorb from others, and to make sense of what is ours and what is coming from the child. It's also hard not to shut down emotionally, so that our ability to receive emotional communication doesn't get limited or distorted.

Stages of containment

Bion described a two-part process that goes on inside someone who is providing containment and an understanding of this process can be helpful in addressing these difficulties. The two parts are called **calm receptiveness** and **active cognitive processing**. Don't let the name of these put you off. In many ways, these two stages are about being able to manage our own feelings enough so that we can hear and feel as well as make sense of what the child is giving to us.

Calm receptiveness: Hearing, thinking and talking about feelings

Calm receptiveness can be thought of as being open to receiving emotional content generally, and more specifically, being open to thinking and talking about emotions. It is a key component of emotional availability.

This is a natural way of being for some, but not so for others and so must be learned. It is unlikely to be natural for anyone who feels they are under physical or emotional threat. When faced with a child's uncontained emotions and the challenging behaviours that can arise at the same time, we sometimes might make the mistake of sacrificing one part of calm receptiveness for the other. On the one hand, we may become unreceptive to the child's emotional communications in our efforts to remain calm. For example, we may become a bit wooden or flat in our responses. On the other hand, we can sometimes become overwhelmed by emotion and lose our ability to be calm as we try to stay emotionally engaged with a child. We may become overcome by anger, frustration, fear or distress alongside the child. Maintaining or regaining our calm and our receptiveness is necessary both for us to avoid a limited or distorted process of absorption, but also to avoid being completely overwhelmed by the emotions so that we can actively process them.

Active cognitive processing: Making sense of what is felt

Active cognitive processing is the process of thinking that brings the emotional content into consciousness and names it, making it thinkable, 'speakable' and more manageable. Bion's choice of the term 'container' is deliberate, as he wanted to give the sense of a space within which things can be thought about. Sometimes active cognitive processing happens very quickly within an interaction in which absorption is taking place, sometimes it takes the form of conscious reflection afterward, and sometimes both. Consistently reflecting on things after they happen can help you to process things better under pressure, right there in the moment.

This cognitive processing makes it possible to then communicate to the child that you have 'heard' the emotional part of his communication. Again, sometimes this can be a natural process which you may not even notice. For example, when a carer verbally conveys to a tired, cranky baby an understanding that he needs sleep, she is probably making this acknowledgement without a lot of thought or effort. Sometimes, however, active cognitive processing can be alien or otherwise difficult. Some carers are not in the habit and have not been supported to think very much about the emotional dimensions of their work. It can also be difficult because of the intensity of the situation. We may have an instinctive habit of shutting down thinking – particularly thinking about emotional things – when we feel threatened. In such situations, we may either give ourselves over to strong emotion without very much thinking, or we may eliminate emotional content from our conscious awareness, thereby making it impossible to think about it. Moreover, if we cannot think about the absorbed feelings, we will not be able to communicate them back to the child in a more manageable form. This form of communication is sometimes referred to as **empathic acknowledgement**.

Empathic acknowledgement: Letting the child know he has been heard

If we think of absorption as received communication, then empathic acknowledgement is our containing response. It is a form of communication that conveys that we've 'heard'. It involves feeling in that it must communicate care and some level of understanding of the child's emotional experience. Sometimes it involves naming a feeling the child is not fully aware of, bringing about a sense of clarity, validation or relief. This can be done, for example, simply by asking a child if he is feeling left out of other children's games, or whether he is missing his mother. Other times this may be too threatening or difficult, and we may need to be the only one who identifies a particularly painful feeling and simply convey a more general acknowledgement of the child's distress. An example of this is when we offer an observation that we can see how upset the child is about something without offering much detail. It must also be acknowledged that sometimes we may simply get it wrong. Whatever the case, empathic acknowledgement can facilitate communication and reduce feelings of isolation, both of which are key ingredients of containment.

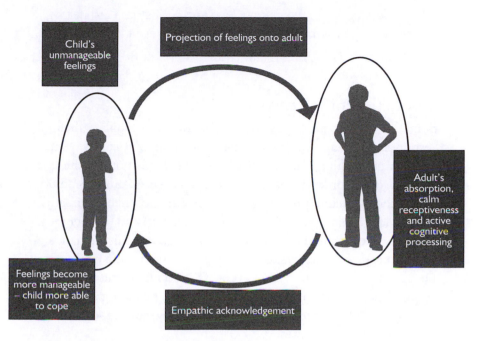

Figure 4.1 The mechanisms of containment

All of the mechanisms of containment sit in the simple but powerful act of tuning in and attentively listening, as described in Chapter Three.

Spotlight on Practice

Dave went outside and found Kevin storming around the grounds. Rather than immediately addressing the destroyed birthday cake, instead he simply observed, out loud, that something had clearly got Kevin really upset and that he was sorry to see it, it being his birthday and all. Kevin looked at Dave with a combination of surprise and suspicion, as he expected to get a row for his behaviour in the kitchen. After allowing for a bit of silence, Dave asked if Kevin was finding it hard to have his birthday here at the school, away from other people he might be thinking about. From there, Kevin began to speak a bit about his worries about his Gran, and that his Mum hadn't been in contact. Given how shaken up Kevin was, and how early into the relationship the two of them seemed to be,

Dave decided not to wonder out loud about whether Kevin felt he deserved to have a happy birthday. Instead, he kept it to himself but actively held it in mind for Kevin.

Containment for carers

Sometimes empathic acknowledgement or similar helpful responses are taught in training packages aimed at carers. While this is a good thing, we want to stress that this is not a technique to be used in order to have effective practice. Calm receptivity and active cognitive processing are necessary to enable empathic acknowledgement and all three are complex and challenging. They are not techniques but ways of being, and this demands a lot from carers. For carers to develop and maintain the capacity to be calmly receptive, to actively process emotional content and to respond clearly and empathically requires significant organisational support. In other words, like the children they care for, carers also need containing processes.

Pause for Reflection

Think of a time when things were really difficult for you – so difficult that you had a hard time thinking clearly. Can you remember what helped you to feel better? Can you remember what helped to restore your ability to think more clearly again? Was there someone who helped in things getting better? If so, can you identify elements of calm receptiveness, active cognitive processing or empathic acknowledgement in how that person helped you?

The work of containment can be complex and demanding. On some levels, providing containment might be relatively easy, natural and constant, but when children's uncontained feelings and their related behaviour are disturbing or otherwise distressing, carers need support to make sense of and manage what they absorb. This is necessary for a number of reasons, the most obvious being the disruptive effect of children's strong, uncontained emotions (and related behaviours) on those who care for them. If the carer cannot process the feelings due to her own feelings of being overwhelmed, it is much harder to respond empathically. Over time, the impact of intense, unprocessed emotions, particularly distressing emotions, can have a harmful effect on carers, and their reactions to the children they care for can become harmful too.

However, even carers who seem able to handle the difficult patches and rarely feel overwhelmed also need containing processes. Lower levels of anxiety or other unprocessed feelings also disrupt our clear thinking, and this disruption can affect individual care practices and organisational functioning. Reflective practices are one way carers and organisations can support the processing of emotions and experiences, and there is growing consensus about its central importance in the provision of good care. Gillian Ruch (2008) has identified clear links between containing processes and the ability to reflect, and has offered a model of containment for carers. It is made up of three parts: feeling containment, doing containment and thinking containment.

Feeling containment for carers

Feeling containment for carers is about *helping to make the work more manageable on an emotional level*. It makes emotions and experiences more 'thinkable' and creates a safe space for them to be expressed. Empathic acknowledgement is a key component of feeling containment, and it can be conveyed through very simple gestures of support, like words of encouragement or even facial expressions. A cup of tea or well-timed humour can be forms of feeling containment, making things feel that bit more bearable. It should also happen in more formal ways, like in regular supervision. Feeling containment can become a core part of organisational culture, happening all of the time in informal, formal, planned and unplanned ways.

For carers who are not in the habit of acknowledging feelings, perhaps because they have been led to believe that it is unprofessional or a form of weakness, feeling containment might seem unnecessary or even risky. Some carers might have been given messages that they should manage their own emotional needs and that looking for organisational support is a sign of inappropriate dependency. We know, however, that supporting carers to acknowledge their professional needs does not foster dependency. Rather, it promotes professional autonomy. This is because feeling containment decreases a carer's need to defend her own competence and emotional survival, which then frees up her focus and energy for meeting the needs of children.

Doing containment for carers

Doing containment for carers is about *clear organisational policies, procedures and expectations that serve the aims of care*. Such clarity can reduce unnecessary anxiety by giving a sense of boundaries and a point of reference.

For organisational policies, procedures and expectations to be containing, they cannot compromise the fundamental aims and principles of good care provision. They also must not become the overriding focus of an organisation's attempt to meet the needs of its carers at the expense of the other forms of containment. When this happens, doing containment becomes counterproductive. This can take different forms: hiding behind paperwork to avoid engaging with children, attempting to simply follow procedures rather than exercise professional judgement or even using an interpretation of policy to support poor practice are all examples. Without support to manage and make sense of the often difficult emotions brought about in caring for children, carers are much more vulnerable to the false certainty that can come from an overriding focus on policies, procedures and organisational expectations.

Thinking containment for carers

Thinking containment for carers is about *providing spaces to support carers to cognitively process the emotions brought up in the work*, but it is about more than this. It is also about *supporting carers to make sense of the trickier aspects of their caring practices* – those areas that are uncertain, controversial or complex. When working with children who have had very difficult starts to life, there can be many such areas. Some examples might include how to respond to a child's sexually harmful behaviour; how to engage with biological parents who struggle to support their child; or even how to respond to a child's requests for loving touch (this last one will be explored in Chapter Eight).

Thinking containment can take place informally in discussions between carers or even in an individual's reflective journal. It is important that it also takes place formally, in protected settings like individual supervision, group supervision and consultancy. Even training can provide thinking containment, but only if it supports carers to make sense of and better understand areas of their practice rather than simply being focused on techniques or the sharing of information.

Thinking containment is the part where you actively process emotions so that they do not overwhelm or remain in the subconscious where they can wreak havoc. Thinking containment also enables open-mindedness and the tolerance of uncertainty, which helps carers to resist the above-mentioned, counterproductive use of policies, procedures and expectations. When we can tolerate uncertainty better, we are more able to notice and have greater creativity in understanding and responding to children.

Relationship and containment for carers

Feeling, doing and thinking containment are all necessary for carers to experience good containment, and the thread that runs through them all is relationship. It may be easier to see that the forms and processes through which feeling and thinking containment happen are relational by nature, but doing containment perhaps warrants further explanation. While a policy or procedure may seem separate from relationships, its effectiveness depends on how well it is thought out, communicated, implemented and modelled, and all of these have a strong relational component.

Sometimes a very supportive professional relationship can provide elements of all three forms of containment, and some individuals can become containers (or serve key containing functions) for the organisation. This can arise from deliberate decision-making around which posts people are placed in, or it can happen more informally with certain people naturally and even unconsciously providing containment for colleagues. It is important, however, that organisations do not rely on one or two key individuals to provide all of the containing functions but instead create planned times and spaces where containing processes occur. This is because it isn't just relationships that provide the containment – containing organisations make those relationships much more possible, especially in the face of difficulties and challenge.

Pause for Reflection

What are some of the things that happen within your work that help with the three parts of containment – feeling, doing and thinking? Which parts of containment could be better? What are some things you can do to help bring about related improvements to those parts?

Now with an understanding of what containment is, how it works and why carers need it as much as the children they care for, our last section looks at how carers can provide containment to the children in their care.

How you and others can help

It can be useful to think about containment for children using the same three parts as containment for carers. The difference will be in the ways that feeling, doing and thinking containment happen.

Feeling containment for children

Feeling containment for children is about helping to make things more *thinkable and manageable on an emotional level*, and empathic acknowledgement is key. Gestures and words of support are helpful, whether this takes the form of a cup of tea, sensitive use of humour or even just putting into words what you think a child is feeling. For some children with significant communication impairments, your tone of voice, facial expression and use of touch will be more important than the words you use, but the process of naming feelings is nevertheless important. For other children, learning to 'talk it out rather than act it out' is often the first step in making emotions thinkable, 'talkable' and manageable.

Proximity is something else you might consider when trying to provide feeling containment. Proximity refers to how close or far away you position yourself to a child, and something as simple as this can help a child feel less overwhelmed by emotion. Sometimes sitting a little closer can be of help, and at other times the helpful response will be to give a little bit of physical distance. Also important is where we position ourselves. For example, a child who feels threatened by us might feel safer when we position ourselves slightly lower than him.

Our chapters about tuning in (Chapter Three), food (Chapter Seven), touch (Chapter Eight) and ways to talk with children (Chapter Nine) all have guidance to support you in providing feeling containment.

Doing containment for children

Policies and procedures are part of *doing containment* in organisations; doing containment in homes or units is made up of *structures, boundaries, rhythms and routines*. When established well, these provide a sense of predictability and security for children, though sometimes it can be a challenge to get them in place – particularly with a child who has come from an environment where chaos and/or loose boundaries were the norm. It is important not to become so preoccupied with doing containment that it overshadows the other two parts of containment, as children will have much greater difficulty accepting boundaries and routines when they are not helped to manage and think about the feelings this will inevitably provoke. Chapters Five, Nine and Ten offer more discussion on the whats, whys and hows of rhythms, routines, limits and boundaries.

Thinking containment for children

Thinking containment is about helping children to *make sense* of their experiences and emotions. This can be what's happening in the moment, or it can be about past events – or sometimes it can connect the two. Talking things through is the most obvious way of providing thinking containment, but it can take other forms as well, including writing, life story work, use of recordings, drawing or other forms of creative expression. Chapter Six, Memory Keepers, will give further guidance about the specifics of this kind of work. Children with significant learning disabilities can be supported to understand events or circumstances through the use of Talking Mats, **Picture Exchange Communication Systems** or other tools to aid communication. For those who have great difficulty with changes to their routine, helping them to make sense of things in advance of the change is an important way to provide thinking containment.

Some children may feel threatened by or are unfamiliar with being invited to think about their feelings and experiences. They may be used to being around adults who have had a limited capacity for this kind of reflection and who may not have encouraged such reflection in them. In such circumstances, it will be important to take things slowly and focus on providing feeling containment to help them become able to do thinking containment. Sometimes a way to start is to let a child know what sense you are making of circumstances, how you feel about it and how you think he might be feeling. This gives the child access to what you are thinking, reducing fears and mistaken assumptions, and it demonstrates your commitment to understand.

Pause for Reflection

Think of a recent time that a child you care for has struggled to manage his feelings. What were the supportive words or gestures you used to help? Looking back, what do you think he was thinking and feeling (it might help to think about what you were feeling)? Did you acknowledge that feeling? If not, how might you have? What did you do, or what might you have done, to help him make sense of his feelings and the situation?

Everyday things you might like to try

Whether for individuals or organisations, containment isn't something that is achieved, once and for all. It is a dynamic process and the degree of containment can vary a lot over time. So if you work in an organisation that does not feel very containing, there are still things you can do.

- Cultivating relationships with fellow carers where it becomes *normal to talk about feelings* is a good start. There is a danger here of getting stuck, repeatedly going over negative emotions in such a way that emotions are not really processed and not much sense is made of anything. Keep an eye on whether or not the conversations you have in these relationships improve your understanding and help you to feel more able to manage what you are experiencing.

- *Bring information about containment to supervision, link worker meetings or team meetings.* Begin to talk about related ideas with a view towards making it normal to regularly discuss the uncertain, controversial or complex areas of practice and the related feelings they provoke. It might be useful to consider that those in management positions also will experience uncontained feelings that make clear thinking difficult, and this makes it difficult to provide containment to their carers. At the end of the day, however, it is the organisation's responsibility to support their carers to provide good care, and an understanding of containment can effectively inform its related efforts to provide related support.

- Look for opportunities to provide **symbolic containment**. Sometimes it can be hard for children to deal with your containing words or actions. Allowing them *opportunities to feel that sense of being contained*, even indirectly, can help. You might want to offer them a cosy blanket to wrap themselves up in or hold the back of the chair while they are talking. Smaller children might be more accepting of being physically held but the blanket can do wonders for older children and can help them feel that sense of being enclosed and contained.

- Notice the things children do for themselves in order to feel contained. Acknowledge them and where possible, support them. A few examples include:

  ○ hiding under tables, beds or blankets

  ○ building dens – outdoors or indoors with cushions from the settee; using a small tent as a 'go to' place when upset can work wonders

  ○ seeking weight or pressure, like wrapping up tight in curtains or lying under a large, cuddly toy

  ○ locking the bedroom or even just taking a bath.

- *Name feelings with empathy* and avoid common phrases that tend to disrupt containment. For example, saying something like 'I can see you're really upset!' is more likely to start a process of containment than 'Calm down!' or 'Stop it'.

- *Recognise when children push limits that this is often a form of asking for containment.* For example, a child who tells you he is going to run away may be asking you to stop him. Let the child know when you see it happening; for example, 'you really want me to say "that's enough"'.

- *Encourage your child to write, draw or use other creative forms of expression, and consider doing so yourself.* Make sure necessary supplies are made available.

Conclusion

Containment is a useful way to think about how to create and maintain a healing home. This chapter has explained what it is, how it works, why it's important, and how you might provide it for children and seek it out for yourself. Understanding and actively engaging in containing processes can support your efforts to do many of the things described in the upcoming chapters, and make them feel far more manageable.

Further reading and resources

Ruch, G. (2008) 'Developing "Containing Contexts" for the Promotion of Effective Work: The Challenge for Organisations'. In B. Luckock and M. Lefevre (eds) *Direct Work: Social Work with Children and Young People in Care* (pp. 295–306). London: British Association for Adoption and Fostering.

Steckley, L. (2010–2011) 'Constrained, Contained or Falling to Pieces?'; 'Containing the Containers: Staff Containment Needs in Residential Child Care'; and 'Containing the Containers II: The Provision of Containing Processes for Staff in Residential Child Care.' *CYC-Online: The International Child and Youth Care On-Line Journal*, November and December 2010; March 2011. Available at: www.cyc-net.org/cyc-online/cyconline-nov2010-steckley.html; www.cyc-net.org/cyc-online/cyconline-dec2010-steckley.html; and www.cyc-net.org/cyc-online/mar2011.pdf#page=59(all accessed 7 August 2015).

For information about touch and containing environments go to:

www.iriss.org.uk/resources/
saia-2011-why-attachment-matters-please-touch-laura-steckley-part-1

www.iriss.org.uk/resources/
saia-2011-why-attachment-matters-please-touch-laura-steckley-part-2

For information on Picture Exchange Communication Systems go to:

www.pecs-unitedkingdom.com

5

Rhythms, Routines and Rituals

Introduction

Parents, carers, child care professionals and social workers often speak about the need for children to have 'healthy routines'. A 'lack of routine' is regularly mentioned in social work reports as a sign of poor parenting. Routines are believed to provide children with a sense of safety and predictability. Often social workers and child care professionals believe that a lack of routine contributes to erratic or 'out of control' behaviour, impulsivity and difficulties in integrating socially. Consequently, many carers see the establishing of healthy routines around sleeping, eating and bathing as one of the first tasks in a new placement. As an experienced residential worker explained to Autumn, '...once the young person is in a routine they become more settled, you can then begin to tackle some of the bigger issues like relationships with family and peers'.

However, establishing routines can be difficult for many of the children who come into the care system. Carers can find children's behaviour volatile and challenging, particularly during times of change and transition. In addition, routines can sometimes be overly rigid, making it harder for carers to make sure there is time and space to do things differently, have fun and be a bit more relaxed. This requires being able to be flexible and works best when there is an easy exchange and rhythm to our relationships with children.

This chapter explores the importance of rhythms, routines and rituals for children. It will examine how an understanding of rhythmicity is crucial to the development of nurturing routines in a variety of care settings and will answer some important questions that carers often raise:

- How can I help a child or young person who seems so 'out of sync' with others?

- What is the best way to introduce a new routine?

- What should I do when children resist or challenge new routines?

- How can the routines and rhythms of daily living be made therapeutic for children who have missed out on early nurture?

The importance of routines, rhythms and rituals

As we saw in Chapter Three, a range of theorists have highlighted that an experience of attunement and reciprocal connectedness is crucial to healthy child development. Parents who are sensitive and responsive to developmental needs get into a 'rhythmic groove' with their child, responding in a timely way and avoiding distress by providing a routine that is predictable. This sense of safety and security is crucial to healthy development across all the domains, and experiences of rhymicity and routines play a significant role in forming it. Opportunities for repeated experiences shape and organise our view of ourselves, our world and even our brains.

Getting into sync is so important that some have argued that this is the defining characteristic of relationships themselves.

The rhythms and routines of caring interactions are sometimes described as intuitive or instinctual. For example, when babies are distressed most parents rock and cuddle them in a rhythmic, affectionate way. They might sing soothing songs or lullabies. This instinct to comfort using rhythmic touch or sound relates to the pulsing quality of the human body: the rhythm of our heart pumping blood through our bodies, our circadian rhythms regulating times for waking and sleeping, and hormonal rhythms influencing processes of maturation and reproduction.

Perhaps we crave routine because we are rhythmic creatures, but whatever the case, routines appear to be one of the ways we establish predictability and organise family life. The common-sense idea that most carers have about the importance of routines is well supported by research findings, which repeatedly show children's outcomes are better when they live in nurturing, predictable environments with healthy routines. We are also learning more and more about the negative impact on children who do not have experiences of nurturing rhythms. We know, for example, that one of the reasons many children find living with parents who have drug or alcohol issues so difficult relates to the unpredictability and lack of routine of family life and the stress this causes. Similarly, some children whose parents suffer from mental health problems have also highlighted the stresses and unpredictability of daily living when a parent or carer is unwell. In these situations, children often take on the role of carers, trying to bring some predictability to their lives and meet the needs of their siblings. It is important to remember that this is not always problematic. With the right support, some caring responsibilities can develop the child's resilience and help her manage and better understand her parents' experience.

The day-to-day rhythms and routines in your home or unit may be new and unfamiliar to children when they come to live with you. Despite our attempts to be caring and establish new routines, the child may feel disoriented and even frightened by this change of rhythm. Such experiences of care may highlight for her what was different or lacking when she was with her birth family or other carers. Explaining her experience of care, one young woman told us about how all the new rules of the residential unit just made her miss her mother even more because they were so different to what she was used to.

Children and young people may find it difficult to adjust to new rhythms and routines, but many of the children we have known have also said they find these helpful. As one young person told Happer *et al.* (2006, p.22):

> *There was more of a routine. At home there was no routine at all. I mean, you just dragged yourself out of bed and went to school, no breakfast or anything. In care...you got up and had a wash and you got dressed, your clothes were pressed for you and everything. And it was clean. Everything was perfect almost. You got pocket money. It was only 50p or something but still...yeah, it was different and it was good.*

Routines can provide children who feel jumbled up and scared on the inside with important **anchor points**. Anchor points refer to the everyday expectations in the home or unit. It is a moment when the carer and child can stop and focus on something specific together; knowing that these points are coming can be reassuring and comforting for the adult and child.

What we do together *regularly* helps to bring us together and helps us to feel part of something bigger then ourselves. It can also help children to tell a story about themselves and who they are. Explaining his life with a new foster carer, one child, Sam, explained to Autumn: 'I help David with our garden. I am good at gardening.' This little boy spent regular time in the garden with his foster carer and enjoyed this very much. It was something they did most Saturday mornings, and helping with this task made Sam feel important and special. It also became an important part of how he described himself ('I'm good at gardening'), it was a new thing he liked doing and felt good at. Therefore, routines also provide children with a sense of the collective and the shared.

Routines around eating, sleeping, watching certain programmes on TV and doing particular chores or activities provide a rhythm to our life as a family or residential group. However, the rhythms of family or community life are about more than routines, they are also about the flow of day-to-day interactions between people. As we saw in Chapter Three, responsive carers find ways to 'tune into' children and young people, looking out for cues and opportunities in the course of the day to engage with the child and understand her feelings and needs. Many carers describe how opportunities for this 'tuning in' and engagement often arise during seemingly mundane and routine activities like watching TV together.

Spotlight on Practice

Autumn was watching MTV with Meagan, a 14-year-old young woman, and a song came on that Meagan really liked. The video depicted women wearing dog collars being led around by the man singing the song. Autumn reflected on this with the young woman, engaging her in a conversation about why she liked the song but also sharing her own feelings about how the video made her feel a bit sad. A conversation about men and women and expectations and double standards around sexual behaviour developed. This was an important topic for this young woman as her social worker and other carers had concerns about her relationships with older boys. By responding to Meagan's interest in discussing this music Autumn also found an opening to talk about a topic that worried her as a carer. The conversation developed naturally from spending time together rather than being forced on the young woman. As time went on watching MTV together became a really important key-time activity for Autumn and this young person and there were many mutual jokes that arose from their reflections on things they talked about during this time. You may have heard this way of engaging with opportunities for learning during the everyday rhythms of life referred to as life-space or opportunity-led work.

Although adults have an important role in shaping the routines and rhythms of family life or group care environments, to have a *healing* impact, rhythms should not be set in stone or dictated.

There should always be a flow back and forth between the people living together and a chance for children and young people to shape the rhythms and routines of daily living. Sometimes children also need a chance to be 'in charge' and there should be a bit of give-and-take to interactions. One carer talked about a child she worked with who instituted 'pyjama pizza night' once a month. The tradition arose out of something she had seen on TV but also related to something she had done with her grandmother when she lived with her. Her foster family went along with this and everyone wore pyjamas to dinner once a month. The girl felt proud that this was something she had 'given' the family, and the experience of being allowed some control and decision-making over adults also made her feel powerful and important. This was helpful for her developing a sense of self-efficacy; she was able to experience herself as a person who can make things happen in the world.

Pause for Reflection

Think back to your own childhood. What rhythms and routines were important? Were there ones that gave you a sense of comfort or security? Were there ones that felt constricting? How did they influence your relationships with the people you lived with? How do you think these experiences have influenced what you do as a carer?

This new routine could be described as a new 'family ritual' for this child and her foster family. We often think of rituals as something solemn that relates to religious festivals, deaths or births. However, many families have rituals around holidays or the change of seasons. Like routines, rituals can be important to the story of our family or our home. When you speak to children and adults about holidays, you inevitably hear about specific rituals like carving pumpkins, opening a present on Christmas Eve or eating a specific kind of food. Creating new rituals with children and young people and helping them find their role in existing family or group rituals can be a key part of helping children and young people to feel included in their new care environment and can help develop a sense of belonging. It can also be the stuff of precious memories they will carry with them. Chapter Six looks in more detail at the impact of creating memories for children.

Spotlight on Practice

Charlie had a ritual of reviewing pictures and objects he had from his mother on the anniversary of her death every year. He often ran away and got into more trouble in the weeks leading up to this anniversary. When staff spoke to him about this, he explained how important it was to remember her, but he also found these feelings overwhelming. He said that running away to be by himself let him remember her. Staff wondered if running away also helped him not feel the feelings about his mother because he was too busy being scared and excited. It seemed as if the running away had also become a ritual. Over time, the residential staff team members were able to talk to him about how he felt about his mother. They were also able to better support him during this time by giving him more individual attention and helping him to develop and collect his memories in a special box and book. Together, they developed a new ritual of going into the countryside on the anniversary of her death so that he could still experience getting away without having to run away from them.

What you may notice

Children who have lived without regular routines are likely to have lived with fear and uncertainty. Unpredictability may have become the norm for them and their energies will have been diverted into figuring out what's coming next. As a result, they may have missed out on other more positive physical, social, emotional and cognitive developmental opportunities. They may struggle at school and in a range of social settings because they don't know how to engage or 'get in sync' with others. They may resist the routines and rhythms of their new home because this new way of living is unfamiliar and, therefore, frightening, and because their experience of adults has taught them to be distrustful.

Some children who have experienced abuse or a significant trauma (such as the sudden death of a loved one) may also struggle to settle down physically and emotionally into a new placement. You may notice that they seem very watchful or pace about. These children may be exhibiting signs of **hyper-arousal** and **hyper-vigilance**; these are terms that psychologists use to describe children whose bodies and brains are continually anticipating potential threats from people or their environment. This may be because they have learned over time that they need to be ready to respond to threats or hurts at any time – their bodies and brains are stuck in a 'fight or flight' reaction. Every new experience and person is weighed up in anticipation of a new potential hurt.

Sometimes children can have flashbacks to their experiences of trauma. A flashback can occur when something in the present, often something very mundane like a smell, sound, object or a look, triggers a memory that unconsciously the child is trying to keep hidden or protected. However, a flashback is more vivid than a normal memory; it can feel to the child as if the traumatic event is actually taking place again. This will trigger a physical and a psychological response. The physical response could include becoming out of breath, a raised heart rate, sweating and physically hitting out or physically folding in on herself. The child will be having lots of difficult thoughts, often about how she is bad or that she has caused this to happen. She may be very afraid she is going to die.

Emotional, physical and sexual abuse often happens in bedrooms and bathrooms during 'normal' routines for the child and such abuse may even have been part of the child's routine. So carers need to be aware of this and be able to respond sensitively if seemingly 'normal' routines cause unexpected reactions in a child. First and foremost, the carer should try to re-establish a sense of safety. They should do this by gently helping to pull the child back into the present moment, reminding her where she is and that no one is going to hurt her here. A comforting toy, special music or even the distraction of a loved television programme may help to anchor the child. Once the child is calm again, it can be helpful to reflect on what has just happened. It is important to discuss these kinds of incidents with other professionals and ensure that long-term plans are in place to help the child to make sense of these experiences and move on.

What you may feel

Many carers describe how exhausting it can be to work with children who have experienced complex trauma. Establishing routines when a child is resistant to this is wearing and takes patience and determination on the part of the carer. It is worth remembering that all of this is pretty tiring and wearing for the child too.

You might feel as if your own rituals and routines are being disrupted and, in turn, you might feel disorientated, unsettled or annoyed. For some people, this level of disruption can result in an emphasis being placed on getting the child to respect the way things are done. It can be difficult to stop and think about the pain that the child is bringing, the previous experience of family life and routine and the uncertainty about the future. Sometimes, routines have to be let go of, or loosened initially until a way of being together can be found. For the adults, this can feel disempowering and can raise worries about control and boundaries. This is an ideal topic to take to supervision or team meetings to fully explore what need to remain as anchor points, and what can be adjusted or loosened until relationships become more established.

How you and others can help: Introducing and maintaining caring routines and new rituals

Ways of 'getting into sync'

Getting into sync with a child starts by spending time getting to know her. It is crucial to find time and space from the beginning of the child's placement where you can really engage with her. This needs to be on the child's terms as much as possible. Where does she feel safe? What does she enjoy doing?

Spotlight on Practice

David had mild learning difficulties and had had four placements in 2 years, including two foster care placements and two emergency stays in residential care. When he moved to a new residential unit, his main way of getting a connection with or the attention of the staff was to break things. However, David loved to play football in all types of weather. By playing regularly with him (even without many skills on the part of many of the staff members!), trust began to develop. Games also included lots of 'high fives' and congratulatory pats on the back. All of these gestures helped the staff get into sync with David, to find a rhythm to interacting with him that worked. This made it easier to manage the other aspects of the unit's routines that David struggled with, for example bath time, which had been particularly difficult but, over time, went from a once-a-week activity to a daily routine.

In attempting to introduce a child to a new routine, the first step is to understand her previous experience and how she might be feeling. This will help you to understand how she might view and experience the introduction of a new routine and also allow you to empathise with her fear, anxiety and/or anger. In turn, this can help the adults to be patient when children are resistant and reactive. Resistance can be expressed by outright refusal to do what is being asked or by making the process very difficult and lengthy. Children can be reactive to routines by blowing up any time the carer signals a move in that direction; turning the television off and beginning the bed time routine can be a typical time for outburst of reactive anger.

The next step is to be clear and child-friendly in your communication about 'how we do things here'. Just doing something because you 'say so' is going to be particularly difficult for a child who has learned not to trust adults. Providing a clear explanation of what we do here and why, even for very small children, can help them to begin to understand that these routines serve a purpose and are part of the way we express our care for them.

Pause for Reflection

Consider a child you are working with where there may be an impending change to routine, or the need to change the routine in some way. What is the goal of this change? What do you think the child needs to understand about this? How can you describe to her what is going to change and why? How do you think she might feel about this change? Why do you think she might feel this way? How do you feel about the change? Why do you feel this way? How could you break down this change into a series of smaller steps? What verbal or visual tools might you use to help the child understand?

There should also be some room for negotiating particular routines and giving the child some age-appropriate choices. Remember, sometimes the emotional or social age of your child may not be the same as her chronological age. In addition, you might need to work with the very established routines that your child brings. For example, if, for years, your child had a very late bed time and always fell asleep in front of the television, going to bed earlier in a dark, quiet room all by herself may be very scary indeed. Very gradually making the bed time an earlier time and making it a lovely, nurturing routine would be a good way to get things started. Indeed if things are fun they are easier for everyone.

Family rituals usually evolve naturally over time. Include young people in those that already exist and try to give them a specific role so that they feel part of things as quickly as possible. Encourage sharing of stories about special times in the past so that you are aware of existing rituals from the child's family of origin. Consider if any of these could become part of what you do as a family and if the child would like this.

Finding the right balance between routine and spontaneity can be challenging for carers. It is important to think about the particular needs of the child in your care. For example, some children need set routines more than others. For the child with autism, who can often experience reality as an overwhelming and confusing jumble of people, sounds and sights, set routines and rituals can make life bearable and comprehensible. Children with autism, Asperger's or other disabilities can also find new people and experiences extremely anxiety provoking. Carers describe how this anxiety can express itself through a range of behaviours including pinching, slapping, kicking, biting or hair pulling. Sticking to set routines and making careful plans to introduce changes can reduce this anxiety. Many carers we know have found the use of **Social Stories** helpful for introducing or enhancing routines with children who do and don't have disabilities. A Social Story is a simple, short description of an activity, event or situation. It includes specific information about what to expect in that situation and why, and can help the child prepare for change.

Spotlight on Practice

Jim, a residential worker, was caring for Sam, a 13-year-old boy with autism. Sam was going to be moving to a new school at the end of the summer and Jim wanted to support Sam to cope with this major change to his routine in stages. He decided to write a series of Social Stories to help Sam understand and respond to this change without becoming extremely distressed and anxious. The focus of the first story was to help Sam prepare to meet his new teacher Meagan. The story started with a description of Sam and the situation, which included pictures. It then went on to provide affirmative and directive statements to help guide behaviour. Here is the text only version of the story:

> Sam is 13 years old (descriptive). Sam likes playing with his cars (descriptive). Sam likes going to school (descriptive). Sam has been at St John's school for 6 years (descriptive). Sam has made many friends at St John's including Sally and Bob (descriptive). Sam has learned many things at St Johns including: numbers, letters and colours (descriptive). Sam is ready to learn new things (descriptive).
>
> Greenhill is a school for children Sam's age (descriptive). The school teaches many subjects including: car repair, woodwork and sport (descriptive). Sam likes these subjects (descriptive).

Sam will learn new things at Greenhill (descriptive). Sam will meet new people at Greenhill (descriptive). It takes time to get to know new people (descriptive). Sam will meet some of these new people before he starts going to Greenhill (descriptive). First he will meet Meagan (descriptive). Meagan will be his new teacher at Greenhill (descriptive). She will come and visit him at St John's and meet Sally and Bob (descriptive).

Meagan is a nice person (affirmative). I will try to stay calm when I meet her (directive). I will raise my hand to say hello to her (directive). Jim will be with me and will help me stay calm when I meet Meagan (cooperative).

Jim read this story to Sam over the week leading up to the visit from Meagan. Sam seemed to enjoy reading the story, pointing to pictures as Jim read the text. When he met Meagan for the first time he did not pull his hair or engage in other distressed behaviours.

Everyday things you might like to try

- You might want to try *creating your own small rituals with each child* you care for. It could be that when you first see her in the morning you always greet her in the same way or that on Sundays you make her a drink in bed or in front of the television. These small acts can become special moments that children can predict or look forward to.

- It is worth looking to *see if your child has started to create her own rituals.* Are there things that she always likes to do in a particular way or at a particular time? It can be good to notice and let her know; 'it seems like it's really important for you to go to your room after school for half an hour'.

- Try to find ways of *giving the child experiences of sharing and creating rhythms* with others. Music classes are a very good way of doing this and many local libraries run free *rhyme time* sessions for children and their carers. For older children who may not want to sing in a group, a *family karaoke* session or even just *singing along with the radio* can be fun and give them a sense of shared rhythm. You might want to make the child a special mix of songs they enjoy singing and dancing along to for this purpose and encourage them to make mixes of their own to share with you.

- *Physical movement with others*, including *dance* and *sport*, can help children develop their coordination and motor skills, and give them an experience of reciprocity and shared rhythm. Your child may not be ready to do this with peers so see if you can help build her confidence by playing catch or passing a ball back and forth in the park. Interactive video games, like Just Dance on Wii, can be another great way to have fun and experience a shared rhythm.

- Consider *developing your own routines and rituals for self care*. Carers we have known have highlighted sport, cooking, that Friday night glass of wine and girls' nights out as essential to their survival as a carer.

- Try *breaking with routine* and see what happens. How do you feel? How do you think the child feels?

Conclusion

It is important to remember that children can and do recover from very extreme experiences of neglect and abuse. Some may benefit from formal therapies but many children may not want this level of engagement or be able to access them. As we have seen in a range of examples throughout this chapter, much of the change that happens for children takes place during ordinary time together. Repeated experiences of care that are safe, responsive and loving give the child the security she needs to explore and develop. These experiences of reliable nurture can help the child learn that the world can be a safe place and that she is a precious and important part of that world. These new perspectives of self and others can, over time, change the way she sees and responds to the world. Be reassured that there is therapeutic value in the day-to-day work you do to get to know and understand a child, communicate compassionately, provide healthy routines and develop rituals that foster a sense of belonging and identity.

Further reading and resources

Attwood, T. (2002) *Why Does Chris Do That?: Some Suggestions Regarding the Cause and Management of the Unusual Behaviour of Children and Adults with Autism and Asperger Syndrome.* London: The National Autistic Society.

Keenan, C. (2002) 'Working Within the Life-Space.' In J. Lishman (ed.) *Handbook of Theory for Practice Teachers in Social Work.* London: Jessica Kingsley Publishers.

Maier, H.W. (2004) 'Rhythmicity: A powerful force for experiencing unity and personal connections.' *CYC net,* Issue 66.

Malchiodi, C.A. (ed.) (2015*) Creative Interventions with Traumatized Children.* London: The Guildord Press.

Perry, B.D. and Szalavitz, M. (2004) *The Boy Who Was Raised as a Dog: And Other Stories from a Child Psychiatrist's Notebook.* New York: Basic Books.

The Children's Society (2011) 'Supporting Children Who Have a Parent With a Mental Illness. Information for Professionals.' Available at: www.youngcarer. com/sites/default/files/mental_illness_booklet_2011_2nd.pdf (accessed 21 March 2014), p.12.

For more information on writing Social Stories go to:

www.autism.org.uk/living-with-autism/strategies-and-approaches/social-stories-and-comic-strip-conversations/how-to-write-a-social-story.aspx

6

Memory Keepers

The Role of Carers in Keeping Hold of the Child's Story

Introduction

The story of a person's life is rarely straightforward. Most lives have various twists and turns, characters that enter and leave, others who remain. There may be some parts filled with rich detail and others that contain only blank spaces or sketches of memory. More often than not, the telling of our story highlights that we have gaps in our knowledge of our own history as well as lost memories, confusions and contradictions. This much is also true for children in looked-after care and for the adults that they become. However, unlike many of us, these children and adults have fewer, if any, people to help them remember, to fill in the gaps or to help manage the contradictions.

As carers, you may be with a child for a brief moment in her life story or for a significant period of her childhood. Either way, your involvement in her life means that you both contribute to her story and help keep the memory of her past experiences.

This chapter explores the importance of holding and sharing memories with children, and discusses practical ways that carers can fulfil this vital aspect of the fostering and residential care role. In particular, it hopes to answer these questions:

- Why do records matter?
- What kind of information should carers keep?
- How should records be kept, stored and shared?

The importance of keeping memories: Why memories matter

There is increasing evidence to suggest that the way in which we know about and understand our lives is crucial to our sense of who we are. It is not so much what has happened to us but how we have made sense of our life and how we are able to talk about it that matters. This not only contributes to our long term sense of self, but also to our capacity to make and keep relationships and to cope with adversity and change. Having a clear sense of who *we* are and where we have come from also influences our ability to support others in developing a robust sense of who *they* are.

This idea of who we are, what some refer to as 'sense of self', begins while a baby is still in the womb. The baby is being sent powerful messages about her place in the world. Ideally, she is welcomed, soothed, spoken to and connected with. As soon as the child is born, verbal and non-verbal messages are being sent and received about who she is and how others feel about her.

Pause for Reflection

Think back to the most recent time that you spent with a baby. It doesn't have to be your own. What messages were being sent to the baby about who he or she is? How were they sent? Who sent them? Were there any that didn't make sense to you? How might repeated messages like the ones you saw or heard translate into a sense of self?

These messages form a pattern that, in turn, generates a story about a person which over time becomes internalised and which plays a crucial role in how that person then goes on to view herself and her relationship to the outside world.

Spotlight on Practice

Rudi was a much wanted baby. Throughout pregnancy his parents, Alice and John, spoke to Rudi, soothing him and telling him about the life they would have together. After his birth, Alice and John continued to delight in Rudi. Even after times when they felt tired and frustrated by him, they were able to gaze lovingly at him, to tell him about his talents, strengths and how much he was loved. Rudi's days were filled with words like 'love', 'special', 'treasure', and in the faces of the people who cared for him, more often than not, he saw smiles, deep knowing and acceptance.

As you can imagine, Rudi went on to seek out experiences that confirmed this sense of who he was (loving and lovable). When times got tough, he had people to fall back on and support him. He was constantly reminded of times past when he had been successful, had delighted those around him or faced new challenges. In the telling of these stories from the past, Rudi was constantly reassured of his sense of self as inherently 'good', that he was known well by others and that his future self was seen as positive. Lucky Rudi!

It would appear, then, that linked to this sense of identity or sense of self can be more general understandings of the type of person we are. Often these are drawn from the messages given to us about ourselves by others, or by the way in which we ourselves have put together our stories. During this process, we start to create a sense of ourselves as, for example, a sporty person, a disabled person, a lazy person, a friendly person, or as some one who copes/doesn't cope, is aggressive, too passive, difficult or easy. These short-hand ways of describing a person accumulate to produce a set of labels that strongly influence how we see ourselves, and our place in the world.

The idea we have about ourselves, about our identity, is further shaped in relation to, or in comparison with, other people, places or experiences. Many of us will chose to describe ourselves as someone's son or daughter, someone's mother or father, partner, friend or neighbour. For others, their employment role, place of birth or current residence may become a key aspect of their identity, how they view themselves and how they wish others to view them.

However, identity can often be seen as context specific. For example, during a discussion with others waiting at the school gates, Ruth's role as a parent might be more important than her role as a social worker; however, the person she is talking to might be more concerned about her employment identity than her parental one. How others view us, the identity they give to us, is not always under our own control.

What you might notice

How we view ourselves is important when thinking about ways to support children in developing a strong sense of who they are. For many, it may be very important to them to remain a child from a particular area or town, or someone who is from a particular family. For others, their looked-after status, for example, their view of themselves as a 'foster child', may be a central feature of how they know and understand themselves.

Pause for Reflection

How does the child you look after describe him or herself? Are there aspects of identity that you find difficult to encourage or support? How do others view your child? What do they draw on to do that?

Spotlight on Practice

Lewis was 8 when he came to live with Meg and Donnie. Prior to living with them he had been in a shared care arrangement, living part of the week with his mother and the other part of the week in a specialist respite unit for children with disabilities. Quite soon after moving, Meg and Donnie noticed that Lewis would mention his disability whenever he met new people or took part in new experiences. They wondered about whether Lewis had been given a message that people only spent time with him because he was 'disabled'. Their support worker suggested that it might be because disability was something that Lewis viewed as central to his sense of self. Either way, Meg and Donnie used an everyday opportunity to begin to explore this idea. Whilst baking fairy cakes, Meg started to talk about how different each cake was. This allowed her to think about the different ways we can think about ourselves and also how others view us. Together they named each cupcake with different characteristics that Lewis saw in himself or ways that people had described him. What became clear was that Lewis had learned from an early age that the adults who had provided nurturing, responsive care were those in the respite service. He seemed to believe that it was only through his disability that he could access this type of relationship. Meg became more convinced that she needed to help Lewis to think not only as himself as a disabled person but to understand that he was now loved and cared for as his whole self.

To make identity, or sense of self, even more of a challenge, what we don't know we often make up! You are not alone in doing this; indeed, research shows us that we fill in the gaps in our knowledge or understanding. This is primarily because uncertainty is hugely anxiety provoking. The 'not knowing' can be difficult for people to tolerate. Therefore, a way for the brain and body to cope is to piece together what we do know in order to create some kind of story that works for us.

All of this matters in relation to the children we are caring for. For those children who have experienced really hard times in their family life, who have been separated from birth families against the families' wishes and who have experienced a number of different primary care arrangements, their sense of their own story may well have become lost, contested, confused and possibly dismissed. Often those around the child are so focused on the present that they forget to remember the past. Common for children who are looked after are:

- a sense of blame for what has happened

- a belief that they are not 'good' and that they have had the power to destroy relationships

- disagreement between key adults about their story

- gaps in information (especially day-to-day information and memories like favourite toy, songs)

- memories that are extremely painful.

Children and young people can have a range of responses to their past. Some of the children you look after might want to know much more about their early years or why they are looked after. They might want to reconnect with people or places, or go over and over the information that they have with you. Others may feel unable or scared to think about the past. They may have been given messages by adults to 'think of the future' or been told that 'the past is the past'. They may have fears about what might be uncovered or believe that they are the cause of what has gone wrong.

As carers and residential workers, it is useful to be alert to indications that a child is looking for information or knowledge about the past. Similarly, a resistance or denial of the past is also something to talk over with your team or support worker.

Now may not be the right time for the child to think about or remember what life was like before coming to live with you. What is essential is that children feel that they can think with you about these things when they are ready and that you are willing to be alongside them as they do so.

Formal life story work, as well as direct introduction of information about the past, works best with children who have shown a curiosity about their own lives. It is far less effective with children who need to have their version of their story as a kind of emotional shield, as a means of coping. For example, it may be that a child needs to believe that her father was ill and in hospital rather than in prison. The need to hang on to these types of ideas seems to be influenced by a range of factors. For example, children are more able to reflect on and consider their journey if they are in a secure placement where that story, whatever it involves, will be accepted and where the child believes that exploring the mess of it will not alter how she is viewed or change the care that is being offered to her. As Holly Van Gulden (1995) famously said about undertaking work with children on their past, there is no point building houses following an earthquake if the ground is still shaking (we have included her book in the 'Further reading' section at the end of the chapter). Children are no different from adults in that if their current living arrangements are not secure, then that will be their preoccupation. In other words, you need to feel safe in the present to begin to think about the pain of the past. However, it may be important for your child to know that there is a different version of events, whilst at the same time acknowledging that now is not the time to explore this.

Thinking about how your child might let you know whether she wants to continue to explore the past is vital. Getting a balance between promoting the idea that the past can be brought into your life together and that it will not alter your feelings for her, needs to be balanced with pushing her into thinking and remembering experiences she is not ready to explore. As carers, this is about making the past an everyday event, rather than approaching it as specific 'work' to be undertaken.

Particular attention needs to be paid to children who have profound physical or learning disabilities. Often, these children's past, their sense of selfhood and identity, gets marginalised in favour of attending to physical needs. For these children, responding to their story, keeping hold of it and making it come alive to them every day, is essential.

Pause for Reflection

How would you describe your child's sense of identity? What words does she use to describe herself? How do you talk about past hurt or her birth parents? If relevant, how do you talk about your child's disability with her?

How you might feel

It is vital that carers think about the role that they can play in the past, present and future of the child in relation to the formation of a sense of self and identity. In the rest of the chapter, we are going to look at some of the formal and informal ways we can help the child with this key aspect of her development. However, to do this, we have to be willing to work with the unknown, to avoid filling in the gaps with fabricated stories to paint a 'better' picture or one that fits the script that might be being given to the child. More importantly, we have to accept that some of this might be new, painful and challenging for the child. Indeed, it is often the small acts of remembering that cause the greatest pain.

You might feel guilty about not knowing the answers to a child's questions. In addition, other residential workers and carers have talked to us about not wanting to upset the child by telling the truth about what has happened or they have told us that they made up information in order to avoid the child being sad or angry. Typically, this relates to questions such as 'Did my Mum cuddle me?' 'Did my mum love me?' Whilst we may want to answer 'yes' to questions like these, we have to acknowledge that this is something that the child wants to know but that we don't have the answer to.

At times, thinking about the past can feel daunting for the carer. You might be worried about saying the wrong thing or giving your child too much information. There may be situations that you know your child has been exposed to or involved in that feel upsetting to you and which you feel that you don't have the expertise to deal with. Talking this over with your partner, close friends, team or social worker can help to share this burden and help you plan your approach. You need to be given support with how this aspect of care might impact on you and how it may make you feel.

How you and others can help: Being a keeper of memories

Foster carers and residential workers play a vital role in keeping hold of children's memories. Memory is not just a static snapshot that can be shared, or not, with a child. Rather, memories are complicated and dynamic. They move and change over time and in different hands. More than anything, children need to feel that their past, their memories, are not disconnected and kept somewhere else. Rather, their past is a living thing that can be brought into the present at any time.

Pause for Reflection

Think about the last time you spent time with extended family or old friends. What did you talk about? How many times were people, places or experiences from the past brought into the discussion? How did that leave you feeling?

In an ideal world, children would come into your care with a handy computer program listing everything that they had ever experienced and felt. All the important people would be clearly listed and described, and the everyday things that the child had known would be laid out for you to see. Sadly, that is never the case. As substitute carers, we often only have snippets of knowledge, the odd photograph or certificate and, if we're lucky, some information about the circumstances leading to the child being in our care.

However, as carers, we can do two crucial things:

1. We can try to find out as much as we can about the past.

2. We can make sure that we capture and pass on as much as we can about the present.

First, find out about the past. When a child comes to live with you, try to find out about the circumstances leading to her reception into care. It is really useful if you can find out the places she has lived and who she has lived with. It can also be very helpful to find out what age she was when the significant events in her life occurred. It is useful to ask if any formal life story work has been done or if the child has a chronological history. Ask the worker if there is anyone who the child might see as an important person or whether there is someone who knew her well. Is there contact with that person? If not, can there be? For those of us who are caring for children with significant physical or learning disabilities, we may have to contend with histories containing hospital stays and respite placements and multiple people who have cared for our child in the past but who are now hard to track down or who might struggle to remember our child amongst the many children they have treated or cared for.

The big events are more often than not recorded and repeated at children's hearings, court, medical reviews or looked-after reviews. However, throughout the years that we have worked with children they consistently want to know about what we might view as the small stuff. It's the little, everyday things that children want to know. 'What did I look like when I was a baby?' 'Did my mum cuddle me?' 'What did I like to eat?' 'Did I have a favourite toy?' 'What was I good at?' Almost every child that we have done life story work with has also wanted to know the origin of his or her name – who picked it and why.

Finding this type of information can be difficult. More often than not, people will present different versions of things. However, this allows you to do another important thing for your child: record those differences. It is not only the memory that you want to record, but whose version of it is being recounted. So, for example, you might want to say or write down 'Your mum said that your favourite toy was a cuddly donkey called Rainbow.' However, you might also need to record (and gently say) 'Jenny, your social worker, Pat, knew you from being a newborn baby. She said that she doesn't remember you ever having any toys.' It is useful to help children with ways of understanding and stating these contradictions: 'Mummy and Pat's memories don't match. Let's keep them both and see if we can find out more.' The differences in stories and the tellers are a crucial part of the child being able to make choices about the version that she herself wishes to believe. For many children, they will need help to hold both versions in their minds.

Recording information for the future can also create challenges. We need to feel confident that our notes and artefacts are going to be kept safe (particularly if you know that the child you are caring for is going to be moving on from your care). We also need to think about recording in a way that is meaningful and useful. Just as our children are diverse and unique, so are the ways in which we capture information. Useful approaches that work for children regardless of disability or literacy include paintings and drawings, photographs, video clips, voice recordings or symbols (e.g. from Boardmaker, Talking Mats or indeed your own pictorial representations of events or memories).

So, once you have some information, the next thing is to keep it alive. In many families, remembering the past is a feature of daily life; we constantly refer back and forth to times past. Children are often very curious about themselves at young stages: 'Did I always hate tomatoes?' 'What did I do when I was two?' Often, as carers we are left with not knowing and it is important that we let children know that rather than making something up. Understandably, carers can want to give children the best version. Returning to the question 'Did my mum ever cuddle me?', it can be heartbreaking to say to a child 'I don't know. It sounds like you would have really liked her to have cuddled you.' In some ways it's easier to say 'I'm sure she did,' but are you sure? Can you give the child reasons why you think this? It is therefore much better to stay with the uncertainty and shoulder that with the child.

When we do know about events or experiences, it is useful to try to weave this knowledge into the everyday conversation you have with your child. Letting her know that she once went to that park with her granny or that the social worker had told you that she has always loved ice cream makes the child's sense of self before the placement with you feel welcomed and accepted. You might also want to acknowledge a parent's birthday or mark the day that the child was removed from home or came to your care. The aim always is to avoid each placement as being one closed container coupled only loosely to the next like a train. A big part of your job is to help trying to join these pieces together.

It is important that the child's version of events is explored before any 'corrections' are imposed. Often, in the telling of the story, children begin to see patterns of events and begin to ask questions. It is much better that any correction comes from these discussions rather than the child's version being dismissed as inaccurate.

This is also important for those times when children who are no longer in your care come back to you for information. It is important to be honest about your experiences and about what happened. Often, children return to placements that have broken down. Your role is to help the child understand what happened. If a key part of the breakdown was her behaviour, then it's okay to let her know that but always make sure that this is done with empathy and alongside acknowledgement of what it meant for you and your role in it. Later in the book, we consider different approaches to communicating with children, including saying 'difficult things'.

Spotlight on Practice

One young man, Pete, who Ruth was working with, wanted to go back to a foster placement where he had lived with his brother. The placement had ended because Pete had assaulted the foster carer. This was the final straw in a relationship that had been very challenging from the outset. Ruth spent some time with the carer before the meeting explaining what it was that Pete wanted from it.

The carer was able to work with her to think about what had been happening for Pete at that time. In the subsequent meeting, the carer was able to say 'When you lived with me you were having such a hard time. You were so worried about your mum and whether she was safe or not. You thought that it was your fault that you were placed in foster care. You were trying everything you could to get home to her and at the same time you felt so bad and so guilty. Hitting me wasn't okay but I've had time to think about why that might have happened. I'm sorry that I couldn't keep you here with me. I thought that I couldn't keep you safe and stop you from hurting anyone else.'

Everyday things you might like to try

And so, now, today, there is so much you know about the child. It might seem mundane and insignificant, but you know if she likes to have her hair washed, what shows she likes to watch on TV, who she plays with, what she dreamt last night. Try to capture these events, experiences and future memories in as many ways as you can.

- One way of doing this is through **memory boxes**. Into these boxes, try to place not only photographs or important symbols of events (certificates, postcards, etc.), but also write about why they are there in the box and name the people present. Ideally, do this with the child, although this might not always be possible. When you can, make copies. Try to have things in duplicate in case the box is lost or destroyed. If the child then moves on from you, go through the box with the child and with the new carer, explain what it all means and why it has been collected. Often carers and staff keep hold of the 'big things', the standout events. For looked-after children, trying to keep hold of the mundane, run-of-the-mill things that happen is also important. This might be all the information (and the only source of information) they have about themselves and their life at this moment in time.

- But memory boxes and life story books need to be alive. You and the child are *doing* the story, not just dusting it off. *So whereever possible, talk about the past.* Mention the things that you did together. Make referring to the past an everyday experience, like it is for most people. Research has shown that 'collective remembering' is a crucial part of relationship making. Being able to talk together about the times you have had helps to join you. Having a box or a book can be a good way of doing this in a more formal way every now and again. Keep these items around the house rather than locked away for safe keeping. If you are worried that they might be destroyed, make copies and take pictures of important items.

- *Be a detective* – find out about the small things. Talk to the social worker about who might have knowledge of the child and whether you can approach them for information. If not, ask if the social worker can find out on your behalf and provide him or her with a list of questions. Remember, the answer to many of the major events may be in the formal case recordings. Focus your 'investigations' on the everyday things that matter to your child.

- If you feel that your child is settled with you, you might want to think about **sensory memories**. This can work well with children who find verbal communication difficult or who have learning difficulties. First, try to find out about positive memories that the child may have had. Think about the sounds, smells, tastes and touch experiences that these events may have included and think about ways to replicate these. It could be the smell of baby lotion, of cakes baking, or the sound of the wind in the trees. Keep in mind that remembering good times can also bring very powerful feelings. Only once you feel confident that your child wants to continue this type of work should you then move to more painful experiences. Importantly, you are letting the child know that you can share these experiences with her and that you accept her past.

Conclusion

People who care for children, day in and day out, are a treasure chest of memories. Every second you are with a child you are potentially making a new memory. And in this time you have opportunities to help the child to connect with a memory from the past. This is the gift of looking after a child. What memories did you make with your child today? How have you helped her make sense of these? How do they fit with the view she has of her life and of her self?

This chapter has explored some of the everyday ways that we can help children gain a sense of their own story and formulate an identity that will be useful to them and a sense of self which is both accepting of the pain and gaps, but also robust enough to deal with them. There are many, many times in looking after children when it can feel as if you have little power or control over events. How you manage memories, from creating them, to storing them, to sharing them and connecting them to the life before your care is something that you can do right now and something which will make an extraordinary difference to the present and future for your child. What a gift!

Further reading and resources

Rees, J. (2009) *Life Story Books for Adopted Children: A Family Friendly Approach.* London: Jessica Kingsley Publishers.

Rose, R. and Philpot, T. (2004) *The Child's Own Story: Life Story Work with Traumatized Children.* London: Jessica Kingsley Publishers.

Van Gulden, H. (1995) *Real Parents, Real Children: Parenting the Adopted Child.* New York: Crossroad Publishing Co.

This useful overview of supporting children who have been bereaved has some ideas about keeping hold of information or marking significant days:

www.winstonswish.org.uk/wp-content/uploads/2013/10/Activities-to-do-with-a-child-that-h as-been-bereaved.pdf

7

Food and its Everyday Use

Introduction

Ask anyone who has ever been on a diet and they will tell you, food is everywhere! It's so much part of our everyday life that we pay it little attention. When we do think about food it can often be in terms of planning: 'What will we have for tea?' 'What do I need to get at the shops?' Or in relation to nutrition: 'Have the children eaten enough fruit and veg?' 'Should we have takeaway?' In more recent times, increasing concerns about food safety have also led foster carers and residential staff to think about issues around food preparation, risk and the management of food and utensils.

This chapter is not so much concerned with food as nutrition. Nor does it discuss the types of food that children should be eating. Rather, this chapter aims to explore what food, and the things we do around food, might represent to adults and children.

By presenting a range of carers' experiences, it discusses some of the meanings that may be being communicated by children and adults through their use of food and also looks at some of the tensions in relation to key food events, like mealtimes. The therapeutic, healing power of food is examined as well as ideas about ways to harness this power.

The chapter will explore these questions:

- Why is food important in looked-after care placements?

- How can carers use food to help children feel better?

- What might carers and children be saying through food?

The importance of thinking symbolically about food

Food and the things that we do with, and around it, are like windows into the everyday world of looked-after children. How food is bought, prepared, shared, stored and talked about can tell us a huge amount about how care is being given and experienced. The everyday behaviours that happen around food, things that we hardly ever think about, can have a huge impact on how out-of-home care is experienced by children. Put simply, it is the 'drip drip' messages and experiences given to children in daily life that can fill them up with good feelings or which can make them feel as if they are wrong or bad. This is most clearly seen in what happens around food. These everyday, repeated experiences have a huge impact not only on children, but also on the adults who care for them.

The inextricable link between food, feelings and relationships begins from birth. Right from the start, when a baby is feeding he is not only taking in milk as a source of physical nourishment but, more profoundly, he is 'digesting' the 'good parent', the feeling of safety, security, trust and confidence in that parent. This taking in of the external world through feeding equips the child with a sense both of his own 'self' and of the external world. Thus, food in this context symbolises, or stands for, love, trust and predictability and, in the process and experience of feeding, serves as a foundational element of the sense of self. Little wonder then that new parents can feel extremely anxious about their baby's feeding experience. For many, these wider symbolic processes might never be considered at a conscious level but the sense of being a 'good parent' and, in turn, a 'good baby' rely, at least in part, on successful and pleasurable feeding.

For many of the children we care for, there have been significant interruptions to this process. For some, this may have been the result of their own ill health at birth. They may have been separated from their mother to receive medical care and attention and have had very painful experiences of feeding, swallowing or digesting. For others, there have been unpredictable or unresponsive early feeding experiences. As a result, food and sustenance may have been something fragile and difficult to pin down and the pain and distress caused by hunger may have been ignored or punished.

Many children have problems feeding in the early days, weeks or even years after birth but go on to have very positive compensatory experiences in other aspects of their care and nurture. Feeding difficulties alone do not necessarily result in long-term emotional or physical harm. However, our children may have not only faced these early obstacles but have had limited alternative experiences to get over them.

Like new parents of a baby, adults caring for children looked after away from home can come to rely on smooth and straightforward feeding practices as being an indicator of their 'good parenting'. Children accepting the food being offered, enjoying the experience of eating it (often with others) and physically growing and blossoming can be an incredibly powerful reward for carers and a clear message to the outside world that they are doing a 'good job'. By contrast, a child's rejection or spoiling of the food being offered can be experienced by adults at a deep and profound level. Feelings can include fears that the child will become ill or lose weight and therefore not only is the child harmed but also the carer may be regarded as having failed in her duties. Rejecting and spoiling behaviour can also become entwined with concerns about the child's lack of acceptance of the 'good care' experience being offered and what this might mean for her and the carer. For still others, children rejecting or spoiling food can be felt as act of defiance, of resisting the boundaries set by adults. For many carers, this can lead to fears of losing control of the child.

Pause for Reflection

Think back to when you were a child. When you think of food in your childhood what comes into your head? Was there an important person preparing or giving you food? Were there particular smells or tastes that you remember? How did making or eating that food make you feel?

For children coming into your care, the experience of being fed consistently and with new routines and expectations can be confusing and destabilising. Some children may have had to source their own food or may have been relied upon to be the provider rather than the receiver of food. The food you offer, like the approach to care itself, can feel alien, unrecognisable and threatening. This consistency of routine can be experienced as oppressive and controlling rather than reassuring and predictable. Children have reported feeling anxious about knowing what to do around food and being exposed as not able or competent. Trying new foods or new ways of preparing and eating food requires confidence in the self as well as others. For many of the children being looked after, this does not come readily.

Accepting the food being offered by carers and what, for some children, are new ways of 'doing food' can be the last tie to be severed between them and their old lives and relationships. The act of acceptance of a carer's food can feel to some children like an act of betrayal. The sense of loss and of difference can be most acutely felt in the sensory experience of 'new food'. Memories remain of a parent or grandparent in a taste or a smell that children can try desperately to recreate. They can demand of carers the 'same macaroni' or 'soup like my granny's', but rarely is it as good.

This powerful sensory memory can also evoke strong 'negative' feelings. Children who have experienced profound neglect or physical, emotional or sexual abuse may have memories or experiences where food has played a part in their trauma. This can be further exacerbated for children who have difficulties swallowing or chewing. They may associate mealtimes with powerful memories of choking or struggling to chew or swallow. Some children with disabilities have recalled mealtimes as being pressure points in their care experiences, both with birth families and in substitute care. The very real risk of choking, infection (if tube fed) or physical pain can have a significant impact on how children and adults react and behave around food.

Unwittingly, carers can stumble into powerful, visceral memories and experiences purely by providing a particular type of food or expecting a behaviour or ritual around that food that represents something quite different for that child. One child who Ruth worked with was punished by his father by having his food spoiled with large amounts of salt. This boy found it hard to eat with others present. He was constantly vigilant to the risk of his food being spoiled and would prefer to eat away from others, often away from the house.

The giving and receiving of food is central to relationships in most cultures. Understanding how to manage in these social situations, what to do and how to behave can mark you out as an insider or outsider. Participation in shared rituals around food can create and maintain a deep sense of belonging and acceptance. Each family or group will have their own behaviours linked to food that become part of the ritual and routine of family life. These rarely have to be discussed or described. Rather, the people involved just seem to know what to expect and how to behave. In some families this might be the expectation that everyone sits together at a table to eat; for others, it might be that the children do the washing up or that the food is served by the mother. Special occasions in families might be marked through the use of food; even small occasions like regular Friday night takeaways or bigger ones like breakfast in bed on birthdays. Those people taking part in these food behaviours understand the meaning of the food in this particular context and, perhaps most significantly, share this meaning with others in the family or group.

This can be particularly difficult for some disabled children who can be excluded from these more relaxed, informal ways of eating. Feeding can take on medical significance, for example, in children who are peg fed or who need special types of food to allow them to swallow (e.g liquid diets). For others, the change in routine or flavours can cause significant anxiety and distress. As carers, we need to think carefully about how we can create these family food rituals in ways that are inclusive.

Pause for Reflection

What happens in your household when someone is ill? Is food eaten in a different place or in a different way? Is the type of food different? Food can also be used to mark time or as a treat. Is there anything you do in your family around food that is different at weekends than during the week?

These rituals, routines and shared meanings can take a long time to establish. This can be challenging for carers and residential staff, who are keen to welcome the child and make him feel at home. Most often, the way in which we do this centres around food. It can also be difficult if your own routines and ways of doing food are challenged, disrupted and changed. However, it can sometimes take that to create a shared new set of routines around food.

Spotlight on Practice

During a training workshop that Ruth was involved in, a carer, Jane, talked about how important she felt it was that the foster children coming into her home obeyed her rules around food. She wanted the children to eat fresh, healthy food and to eat only at the table. Jane viewed the coming together at mealtimes as essential to building a sense of connection amongst the family and to be together to share experiences. She felt frustrated and angry when the children rejected the food that she had worked hard to prepare and described mealtimes as 'battlegrounds'. She described her sense that her children used food as a way of 'winding her up' and controlling her.

Jane felt the pressure to provide routine to the children, both of whom had had very unpredictable, chaotic lives. Her support worker was concerned about the weight that one of the children, Ben, had put on since coming into her care and had stressed the need for the household to follow a healthy diet.

Once the training group began to talk, we started to think about how some of the pressures that Jane was feeling, and the rules she had set up as a result, might be experienced by the children. We thought about children who had had very limited experience of eating together, of eating healthy food and using cutlery and 'table manners'. Some of the group described children who felt they had no control over most aspects of their lives but that they could control what they ate and where. In addition, food and the eating of food together were seen by many as a very intimate act and one that needed a long time to be established.

So it seemed that Jane and her children were both feeling bad and feeling that they weren't doing a 'good job' of being a carer or a child in the family. Food was standing for, or symbolising, much more than fuel for the body. In this example, food may have been symbolising a range of much deeper thoughts, feelings and beliefs, including control, confusion, nurture, rules, routine, ritual, a way to express feelings and a means of communicating care, resistance or rejection of the placement.

Food, therefore, works not only as sustenance, or fuel, to keep our bodies going but also symbolically. Food can come to represent thoughts, feelings and relationships: often the very things that are the sources of deep emotional pain for those being looked after. Food can be a vital means of *showing* and *doing* care. It is far more successful in communicating care of another than simply *saying* caring words. This is vital to remember when thinking about the opportunities your home provides to children to let them care. This might be care for themselves, for siblings or friends or for you. Food is an excellent vehicle for children to learn how to 'do' care but they need to be allowed to have access to the equipment and food to do so.

Perhaps more challenging is that power relationships between adults and children are often played out and negotiated via food practices; for example, through the contesting of rules for family and school mealtimes. As in Jane's experience, both she and the children were using the food routines, at least in part, to show 'who was boss'.

What it is most important to remember about how food might be being used in your home is that you and the other adults will be using food and the practices around it as much as children. Food is a powerful way to communicate and express a range of feelings and behaviours that we all need to share.

What you may notice

Some children in foster or residential care have few difficulties around food. They seem to understand and accept the rules and routines of their placement around food and can clearly articulate their views and experiences of food, both in the past and in the present. However, many children, and indeed adults who care for them, can find food and what happens around it challenging. Often food is talked about it because an aspect of it has become problematic. Commons worries or problems around food tend to fall into two main categories: children not complying with food-based rules or children's unusual eating behaviours.

As discussed in Chapter Five, rhythms and routines may involve food and these can vary enormously between different carers and residential units. What is often shared is the importance of food being predictable for children. This is valuable in meeting very basic needs around food as fuel, but also as a symbol of consistent, trustworthy adults. However, at times, this much-needed predictability can become more of a regime than a routine, where children are expected from the outset to behave in particular ways around food.

You may notice that the child you are looking after struggles with routine. Children can feel extremely anxious about getting it wrong around food or having to eat in front of other people. Often children are unsure of what they are or are not allowed to have to eat or what is expected of them around food. They can deal with this uncertainty and anxiety in a range of ways, including rejecting, demanding or spoiling food. For some children, accepting the food you make for them can feel like an act of betrayal against a parent. Accepting your food is accepting your care. For others there can be fears about the food being poisoned or contaminated. They might believe that adults like you are not to be trusted or relied upon. Children might grab all the food and find it impossible to share, or they might find it difficult to select or choose. It can be hard for children to know what their favourite food is if they have never been helped to feel they are worthy of having choice or opinion.

You might also see food being used by children in other ways that seem unusual or concerning. Carers and staff often report children hoarding or stealing food. Children can often overeat, apparently never feeling full or satisfied. At the other extreme, carers can worry about children not eating enough. Some carers describe children not eating at mealtimes but wanting to eat snacks or spending their money on 'bad' treats and snacks. Children can be humiliated by adults or even segregated from others because of how they eat. Children who find it difficult to chew, swallow and digest can cause some adults to feel uncomfortable or put off their own food. Adults can also pass on their anxieties about food being eaten too slowly or not properly chewed.

Children may want to use food to show that they care for you or for others in the home or unit. Food can be a powerful means for children to safely communicate to you that you are cared for, known and loved. Food is also a means to show care of the self, paying attention to what is eaten and how it is cooked and prepared. Sometimes in the rush to protect children from 'adult' responsibilities or risk of harm, adults block children's efforts to care in this way. In some institutions, children are not allowed free access to the kitchen, whilst in other foster homes or residential units, children have very limited access to food or drinks.

You might also notice children who are highly compliant around food and accepting of everything that is given to them. For some this may be because they feel safe and secure in the placement and there has been a good 'fit' between the family food practices and the child's. However, there may also be children whose way of coping with everyday life has been to suppress their own feelings and needs, and instead focus on pleasing the adults around them. Such children maintain their emotional and physical safety by keeping their distance. In the short term this can be an effective strategy, but all the while the painful feelings are kept hidden away.

What you may feel

Children and adults use behaviours to communicate, both consciously and unconsciously, their inner thoughts and feelings. Actions really do speak louder than words! Nowhere is this done so regularly as around food. In everyday ways, we use food to express to others how we feel about them, about our situation or about ourselves.

Food can also be a way to keep feelings at bay. We can suppress feelings by stuffing them down with food, or displace feelings by preparing food or feeding others. Early on in Ruth's working life as a social worker, she was involved in some family work with Janie, a young person with learning difficulties, and her grandmother, who had been her kinship carer. Janie was living in a residential unit, but was desperate to return to the care of her grandmother. During weekly sessions, Ruth would be greeted by a spread of sandwiches, cakes, scones and pancakes, all of which had been homemade. The child's grandmother would avoid talking about the situation and how she was feeling by constantly refreshing the tea cups or passing the plates. Nowhere was the ambivalence of care so well articulated through food as here. The grandmother showed her care and love for her granddaughter through this extensive preparation but avoided the pain of the situation in which they found themselves (and the pain of saying that she could no longer be her carer) through food.

As we have already said in the chapter, children's behaviour around food can leave you feeling a range of powerful emotions. These can range from joy and love to rejection, disgust, frustration, hopelessness and powerlessness. The list is endless! What is important is that you reflect on and share these feelings with your support team. Our own food memories are never far from how we think about and react to food. It is therefore important that as part of the reflection on what is happening for you in relation to the child, you also think about what you bring to the encounter.

Pause for Reflection

Taking yourself back again to when you were a child, what were the rules and routines around food in your house? How did you know if you were eating enough/too much/the right food? What happened when you got things wrong around food?

How you and others can help

As discussed in Chapter Five, carers have to pay close attention to the routine and rituals that they have in their home and how a child might experience these. The predictability of mealtimes, of food availability, of taste and flavours can serve as a crucial resource to communicate the much deeper consistency and availability of love, care and support. However, it is always worth reflecting on why such routines exist and whether they need to be adapted during the care of your particular child. Talking as a residential team or with your supervising social worker can really help to think about what function food and the behaviours around it are serving in your home or unit.

Pause for Reflection

What do you want children to feel about your home? How might food be used to communicate that?

Discussions with colleagues and support staff are also vital to explore how behaviour around food is making you feel. If food is being used as a means of communicating, it is essential that we as carers have space and time to think about what is being said to us. Children can share their inner sense of rage, disgust, shame and fear through their food behaviours. Paying attention to this and working with it rather than shutting it down can be crucial in helping children to recover.

Children over or undereating can be a huge source of stress for carers. The child who is never full or who is constantly looking for more and more food may be doing so for a whole host of reasons. For some, this may be the straightforward adjustment to trusting that food will continue to be available, that they don't have to stock up or hide food. For others, having their needs met at any level will be a new experience and one that they will strive to get more of. Children need help to adjust to having their needs met through relationships. It may be that food acts as a bridge to that. If so, it is vital that such food needs are met in an enjoyable and positive way rather than communicating to children that expressing a need is something that will be punished.

Earlier in the chapter we talked about some of the anxieties that might be present for children around food. Coming together to share a meal might be felt as exposing, both emotionally and socially. Eating with others is a very intimate bodily act and, for some children, it can be riddled with fear and discomfort. Having to chat, use cutlery and pass round food can fill children (and adults) with dread. For others, having to be fed by an adult or through peg feeding can be a source of dread, but can also mean that they miss out on what can be sociable and enjoyable times. The pace at which you allow children to join your table is crucial. The table becomes a symbol of 'family' in many ways. Accepting the child, allowing him to have some control over how quickly or to what extent he joins is often beneficial.

It is useful to think about what is most important to you about children at mealtimes. Is it coming together at one point in the day? Is it sharing food together? Is it being predictable? Is it making clear to a child who is in charge? Decide which is the most important and think about ways to make that happen. For example, in one of the Food for Thought workshops, a residential worker talked about mealtimes as important to help children feel connected to the unit and to the staff team. He described that initially, children would often struggle to sit through a whole meal, opting to rush through the food and leave. Over time, children would learn that they could re-join the table and then, at their own pace, would opt to stay at the table, often long after the meal was finished.

For children who are anxious about their food being contaminated or spoilt in some way, it is helpful to recognise that their distrust of food often has its roots in a much deeper sense of mistrust in the providers of care. Although often this mistrust is at a wider level, beyond the actual food experience, there will be some children we look after who will have had real experiences of food being spat on, oversalted or dropped on the floor. Involving children in the preparation of food is a useful way to try to help ease some of this anxiety. It may also be that some children will need a period of time where their food is prepackaged and sealed, and where they themselves can take ownership of removing it from that packaging. This can be very hard in a group care setting or where foster carers are looking after other children. Balancing individual needs with the collective needs of the group is brought into stark relief in the discussion of food.

Perhaps the most important function that food can serve is a tangible way to show that you are really in tune with the child in your care. Offering children a drink or a snack because you notice that they look hungry or thirsty or you know they are hot after playing or need comfort after an argument with their friends is an incredible way to demonstrate attunement. To do this, there needs to be space to act and react to that individual child. For example, attunement requires that we move beyond the routine of food provision to noticing and responding to an individual child at any given moment in time. Any routine needs to be flexible enough to do this; otherwise it is the routine that feels responded to rather than the child.

This attunement relates back to much earlier child development and can be further enhanced by showing, through food, that you have held the child 'in mind'. In other words, even though the child was not with you, you thought about him and thought about what he would need to feel good. Often these powerful symbolic actions – 'I saw this cake and I thought of you as I know how much you like it.' or 'I saw this shiny red apple and I thought, "poor Emma having to sit a maths test, I'm going to have this ready for her for coming home"' – are not necessarily needed nutritionally but are needed emotionally.

Spotlight on Practice

During one of the Food for Thought peer support groups, one foster carer, Paula, talked about her experience of looking after her foster son, David. David had been with her for almost a year. Paula described him as very withdrawn and anxious when he was first placed with her. He would rarely sit at the table and often asked if he could eat on his own. David rarely finished any meal but would hoard food in his school bag and bedroom. Paula and her partner decided that as long as David was eating something, they wouldn't make too big a deal of the way in which he ate. However, slowly over time, David was choosing to eat with the rest of the family and seemed to be enjoying more of the food being provided.

In the few months leading up to the workshop, David had begun to request tinned stew from a particular shop. Paula described herself as feeling disgusted by this food and was unhappy providing it to David. She spoke with her support worker and they agreed that David's wishes in this instance should be honoured and therefore tins of stew were bought. It became clear to Paula that David did not want to have the stew heated. Instead, he wanted to eat it out of the tin. Importantly, he wanted Paula to sit with him as he did so.

Paula was very upset by this experience and wanted to stop the use of the tinned stew. In the group, we thought together about what David might be communicating by this food behaviour. We wondered about David's increasing trust in Paula and whether he wanted to share his past story with her. Perhaps David wanted to make sure that Paula would love this 'yucky' or different part of David? Perhaps he wanted her to go back with him to a time when he had to fend for himself but to re-experience it with someone who cared deeply for him? We also wondered whether the deepening connection to Paula and her family meant that David was trying to keep a link to his past family.

Whatever was motivating David's behaviour, Paula and her family were doing a lovely job of allowing him the space and time to explore and express himself through food. They accepted his need to pace his belonging to the family (perhaps symbolised by the joining the meal table) as well as his need to hoard or ask for special food. Through food, Paula was able to get alongside David and to show him that he was accepted. Perhaps most importantly, by being able to talk and share her own feelings, Paula was more able to contain and have empathy for David.

Everyday things you might like to try

- Feelings about food can be complex and it helps to *know something about the child's food experiences.* Talk about food and food memories with the child; you can also share your food memories, which will help him to get to know you. If there is a special dish he loves, see if he would like to help you buy the ingredients and make it together.

- See if you can *involve the child more in planning and preparing meals.* Smaller children may love helping you choose vegetables and fruit – take the time to smell and touch and talk about the variety of food. Give them tasks in the kitchen and praise them for helping deliver the finished product. Children love opportunities to feel that they are important and helpful to others.

- Sometimes food can be used to help children regain aspects of development that they have had limited chance to experience. One way to do this is to *provide a warm drink each night* before bed. We have found that drinks bottles work really well for this. Their shape and size look similar to baby bottles and they are held and sucked in the same way. Your child need never know that that is why you are offering hot milk or chocolate in this way, but we have seen many children and young people grip and suck the bottle in a way that is clearly linked to much earlier development.

- *Baking* can be a great thing to try with a child. Remember that the purpose of baking will determine the experience so if you have a child who you think has missed out on early sensory experiences, the mixing, squishing and tasting of baking can be useful. The actual cake at the end is less important. This type of baking is likely to be messy!

- For others, they might want to *bake to provide for someone coming*. Again, these cakes might get spoiled at the last minute (this can be for many reasons) and it is important to let that happen and acknowledge it (it was too hard to risk making a nice cake for your Granny). Adults can get caught up in getting it right and forget about what symbolic function the baking might be serving.

- If your child has a disability that involves complex health needs and eating difficulties, talk through your own anxieties and the anxieties/feelings of other family members or people in the residential unit. Don't be afraid to put eating on the agenda as an important and potentially positive aspect of the child's life.

- Think about ways in which you might be able to feed your child and in which he might feed you. This is a great way to develop trust and can be used as a bridge to other forms of touch. This might be done by tasting each other's food or having a bite of a treat.

- *Try reflecting the behaviour* that you are seeing in the child. That way, the child will know that you are paying close attention and are noticing the things that are important to him. You might want to try 'it seemed like you couldn't get enough today' or 'it's hard to stop eating' or 'it's hard to be at the table tonight'. Try to think about what is behind the behaviour.

Conclusion

This chapter has discussed some of the food behaviours that you or your children might be demonstrating. It has suggested that time should be taken to reflect on what is being communicated by you or by the children you care for in how you use food and what you do around food. Food can be a powerful way of allowing children an experience of autonomy and control and of showing love and care and can be used as a means of children telling you about the life they had before coming to live with you. Whilst it is important to think about the nutrition being offered, it is vital to think about what is being communicated through food actions.

Further reading and resources

Barton, S. Gonzalez, R. and Tomlison, P. (2011) *Therapeutic Residential Care for Children and Young People: An Attachment and Trauma Informed Model for Practice.* London: Jessica Kingsley Publishers.

Punch, S., Dorrer, N., Emond, R. and McIntosh, I. (2009) *Food Practices in Residential Children's Homes: The Views and Experiences of Staff and Children. A Resource Handbook for Reflection.* Stirling: University of Stirling.

Warman, A. (1990) *Recipes for Fostering: Sharing Food and Stories.* London: BAAF.

Whitwell, J. (1990) 'The Importance of Food in Relation to the Treatment of Deprived and Disturbed Children in Care.' Available at: www.johnwhitwell. co.uk/index.php/the-importance-of-food-in-relation-to-the-treatment-of-deprived-and-disturbed-children-in-care/ (accessed 7 August 2014).

The Food for Thought project has a useful website that provides a range of free downloadable materials that can be used by residential workers and carers in their work with food:

www.foodforthoughtproject.info

8

Touch

Introduction

Touch is a fundamental part of being human and is best understood within the context of relationships. We experience touch in varying forms throughout our lives. Touching exchanges can be very intense and personal, or can happen in fleeting and unnoticed ways. In addition, there are many different meanings associated with touch; these meanings are personal, based on past experiences, and they are social, based on collective understandings. This chapter will focus on touch as part of your role and will offer some useful information about how it can promote the development of children you care for. It will also address some of the difficulties you may encounter related to touch and what might be done about them.

By touch, we mean any form of physical contact. There are countless obvious and unnoticed ways that people's bodies come into contact with one another. Here are some examples:

- hugs or cuddles
- a light touch on someone's shoulder as we pass by
- functional touch, like that involved in helping a child with grooming or eating
- touch that is involved in play.

This chapter will address the importance of touch in supporting children's development and healing; it will also address some of the negative experiences of physical contact that children have experienced, and those that you might experience in caring for them. In exploring the use of touch in creating a healing home, we will address questions that carers sometimes grapple with, including:

- How can everyday interactions involving touch make a positive difference to children's development?
- How can I tap into the healing potential of touch with a child who is very resistant to being touched?
- How do I respond to a child who is invasive in the way he touches others?

The importance of touch

Research is giving us increasingly strong evidence that touch is not just beneficial in promoting development and healing, it is absolutely necessary. Tiffany Field (2014) wrote an excellent book on touch and has developed a Touch Research Institute that carries out and collects research about touch. Much of what is written here is informed by her work.

Touch and development

Touch is necessary not just for human survival and development; it is necessary for all mammals. We know from research on other mammals that, in infancy, close physical contact of all different kinds contributes to physical growth, weight gain, increased activity, decreased fearfulness, increased resistance to stress and the development of the immune system.

In humans, touch has been connected to the development of the hippocampus – a part of our brain that is involved in the formation of memory and the linking of senses and emotion. It has also been linked with helping to reduce levels of cortisol – a hormone associated with stress. In one study in the United States, doctors increased the amount of skin-to-skin contact between infants and mothers by 6 hours over the first 3 days after birth. One month after birth, they found that these mothers soothed their infants more, fondled them more, made more eye contact and made fewer commands than those mothers and infants who had routine contact. Five years later, the children who received more touch scored higher on tests related to cognitive development than their less-initially-touched counterparts.

One way of understanding these findings is to consider that by increasing the amount of touch at a critical time (just after birth), a stronger foundation was set for attachment and bonding.

When a child experiences a secure attachment, he has a sense of security (as described in Chapter Two) that enables him to explore his world, and this exploration is the stuff of his cognitive and social development. So we can see how touch during early infancy might have an impact on the processes of attachment, which will in turn have an impact on cognitive development.

The processes involved in attachment and bonding necessarily involve touch. These include holding; close contact during feeding, changing and bathing; and physical forms of soothing, stimulation and affection. Research indicates that physical contact with another person can play a significant role in reducing stress and increasing feelings of safety and comfort. Touch is also an important component in the kinds of positive interactions that enable a child to feel accepted and valued, which leads to the development of self-esteem and self-worth. Some children have not experienced enough touch during infancy due to parental neglect. Others have spent their first days, weeks or even months in incubators due to premature birth, foetal alcohol syndrome or some type of impairment.

Pause for Reflection

Think about a child you care for and what you know or suspect with regard to his early experiences of touch. How might these experiences have affected his development of attachment? What about his development more generally? How might they affect how he currently experiences touch?

Touch and communication

So we know that touch is a vital ingredient in children's development; it is also an important component in communication. Indeed, it can be seen as a form of communication in itself. We communicate care, fondness and presence in the way that we physically connect with others. Negative messages are also sometimes conveyed through touch, including anger, rejection or dominance. And sometimes, these messages can get mixed up in touching exchanges, especially when people have a mixture of feelings.

Spotlight on Practice

Kurt has been away on annual leave for 2 weeks. When he returns, he approaches Martin with the intention of giving him a cuddle. Instead, Martin greets Kurt with a swift, sharp punch to his upper arm while laughing and darting away as if playing a game. Kurt is initially irritated but quickly wonders what Martin may be communicating to him via the punch.

Touch and culture

The meanings people make about exchanges involving touch are shaped by their own previous experiences, the cultures they come from and the culture where the communication is happening. So, for example, consider the way that two people greet each other. Depending on the circumstances, this greeting might involve the shaking of hands, the kissing of cheeks, two people hugging or no touching whatsoever. The type and degree of touching will be influenced by culture, by the nature of the relationship between these two people, the previous experiences each of them has had and how they are feeling when they meet.

In some cultures, frequent touching and close physical contact between people is considered natural and normal, whereas in others the same level of touching and closeness might be deemed abnormal or strange. Take, for example, two men holding hands. In some countries, like the UK or the US, there would be a likely assumption that the two men are in some sort of sexual or romantic relationship and, depending on who is doing the viewing (and even the part of the country in which they're viewing), it would be seen as normal and acceptable or abnormal and unacceptable. In Arab countries, however, two men holding hands is seen as a natural expression of friendship or respect and there would be no automatic assumption about sex or romance.

Another cultural element that will affect how touch is experienced and understood has to do with more recent developments in societies' awareness of sexual abuse. There was a time when many adults were far less aware of the prevalence and impacts of sexual abuse and therefore it would not occur to them that their touching interactions might be interpreted in a sexual way. While it is a good thing that our increased awareness enables a greater likelihood of detecting and responding to sexual abuse, an unfortunate byproduct has been a culture of fear that has sprung up in relation to touching between adults and children. In some places, this has resulted in 'no touch' policies or heavily restricted practices and, in many, the habit of touch has become less natural or spontaneous.

Pause for Reflection

Think about a recent time where you used touch to communicate something to a child you care for. What was it that you were trying to convey to him? Do you have a sense about whether he received the message you were trying to convey? How might cultural factors influence the degree to which your intention was understood?

Touch and carers

It is not just infants or children who need touch. Many studies tell us that people experience a greater degree of well-being when they are touched regularly in caring and supportive ways. Our needs for touch for survival and functioning do decrease as we grow through infancy and childhood, but we never reach an age where touch is no longer beneficial. This is relevant not only to the young people you care for, but also to you. The attachment, bonding and communication that happen through touch, when it's working well, promote mutuality, or a sense of reciprocal connectedness in relationship. This experience of mutuality is beneficial to the carer and to the recipient of care. We would even go so far as to say that mutuality in relationships is necessary to help children heal from damage done in previous relationships.

Sometimes, however, past experiences related to touch may make it difficult to experience touch in a positive way. We address some of the related challenges in the next section.

What you may notice

Touch may not be an obvious issue, for either you or the child or children you care for, and so you may not have noticed anything out of the ordinary in relation to it. You may notice the types of touch that a child responds favourably to, whether functional, like hair-brushing or lifting of smaller children, or affectionate, like an arm around the shoulders or a back scratch. You also may notice ways of touching that put a child off; for example, some children really don't like having their face washed. You'll also probably have noticed that a child might respond to the same type of touch in different ways depending on his mood at the time or other circumstances, like whether friends are present. You may have enjoyed some of the positive effects of touch, like feelings of connectedness and mutuality as discussed above. The part of your care involving touch can be very rewarding for all involved, and that's a good thing!

On the other side of the coin, all sorts of things can interfere with touch being experienced as positive. The most compelling and obvious would be previous abuse that involved touch, and such experiences can be relevant to carers as well as children. Touch can come to mean hurt or humiliation, something to be avoided. Carers may worry about triggering bad memories or feelings of insecurity when working with touch-resistant young people. They may also be concerned that their motives to reassure or comfort might be interpreted in a sexual or otherwise sinister way.

So you may notice a child who avoids physical contact, either with adults or with other children. Or, you may notice invasive forms of touch from a child. Some children have experienced insufficient touch in their early years as part of a wider situation of neglect. While some of these children may also resist touch, others will instead seek touch with greater frequency and intensity than what you might experience as 'normal'. Still others will only initiate or accept touch that is aggressive in nature, and it may be that this is the only form of touch that is familiar or tolerable to them.

Children may also touch themselves or others in a sexual way. While this may indicate some form of trauma or developmental interference, it may instead be a part of normal development. Most children become curious about the more private parts and functions of theirs and others' bodies. Adolescence is also a time of renewed interest in sex. Masturbation, when done in private, is a normal, healthy form of self-touch and evidence of such activity should not cause alarm. This is the case whether or not a child is disabled, though it may take more support to help a child with a significant learning or physical disability to explore his own body safely and privately.

Students on social work and residential child care courses have become increasingly interested in touch as a focus for their research projects. Some students interviewed care leavers about their views and experiences of touch and found that care leavers valued forms of reassuring touch from staff, including things as simple as a hand on their shoulder. One young care leaver referred to feeling love for staff because of how they really cared about him and even 'hurt for him' when he was upset. In his interview, he connected feeling cared about with staff giving him a hug and making things feel better. Sadly, physical restraint or staff's responses to challenging behaviour were the first examples given when asked about their recollections of touch in residential care, with one care leaver commenting, 'When I think about staff using touch I think about being restrained'. In a larger study of physical restraint in residential child care, a few young people told Laura that they sometimes got restrained in order to be held while letting out intense anger or while crying. This is a complex and difficult area of care that is discussed further in Chapter Ten.

The way a child engages in touch may tell you something about how he views himself. On a most basic level, some children's use of touch reflects their understanding of interpersonal boundaries – literally of where they 'end' and you 'begin'. A child who touches in a very full on, invasive way may reflect his experiences of 'boundarylessness'; conversely, a child who never initiates or accepts touch may experience himself as completely disconnected from other people or so fundamentally disgusting as to be untouchable.

With some children, you also may notice inconsistent behaviour and 'mixed messages' related to touch. A child may accept and even seem to enjoy being touched some of the time, only to reject touch on other occasions for no observable reason. This can sometimes be related to a need to control the touching encounter; other times it may be that there are triggers – a smell, a phrase or even a slightly different form of touch – that elicit feelings of fear, threat or anger. You may be able to learn what these triggers are for the child, or they may be so subtle that you never come to know them.

Some research links touch deprivation in early life to subsequent emotional disturbances and violent behaviour. Other research links a lack of touch with sleep disturbances, delays in physical growth and inhibitions of the immune system. If the child you care for struggles with aggression or sleep, for instance, it may not be possible to untangle whether this is about touch deprivation, previous trauma or current stressors. The point really isn't to narrow it down to one thing, necessarily, but to think about your child's needs holistically and consider the place of touch within that.

Pause for Reflection

What do you know about your child's previous experiences of touch before you began caring for him? What kinds of physical contact does he seek out? What does he shy away from? How might these observations inform a thoughtful approach to how you integrate touch in your care?

How you may feel

The internal call to reach out and touch another, whether in offering comfort or sharing joy, can be powerful. It is instinctual and part of what it means to be human. You may well experience a myriad of positive feelings related to touch, including love, hope, happiness, contentment, comfort and relief.

As mentioned above, you may also feel apprehensive about touching a young person who is resistant to being touched, or feel unsure about your organisation's expectations of you. You may feel annoyed by a child who touches in a full-on or otherwise unwelcomed way. Or, you may feel confused by the mixed messages conveyed by a child in your care, or by a mixture of contradictory feelings that can simultaneously rise up within you. There's also the possibility of 'spin off' feelings, for example, feeling weak because of the feelings of vulnerability provoked by the way a young person touches you. Self-harm and sexualised touch tend to provoke the strongest negative reactions in carers.

Spotlight on Practice

Laura can remember working with a girl who, in her struggle with past experiences of physical abuse, sexual abuse and neglect, had very different personal boundaries from the other young people she was working with. Laura often felt physically invaded by the way the girl consistently sought her out for hugs and other close contact, and she found it difficult to physically disengage from her. The girl would cling on and wouldn't let go, and sometimes she would touch Laura in a sexual way. The sexual nature of the contact was especially challenging to deal with, and it was compounded by the guilt Laura felt about her own feelings of disgust and rejection towards this girl. In her efforts to not be yet another adult to reject this child, she very likely sent mixed messages in her efforts to set personal boundaries.

Pause for Reflection

Think about the last time you had a strong reaction to an interaction that involved touch between you and a child you care for. How might this reaction relate to your experiences of touch when you were a child? Looking back, what meaning did you ascribe to the touching dimension of this interaction? How might that have affected how you're feeling?

While other dimensions of caregiving carry significant emotional charge, touch often carries the most powerful. This is reflected in the way our society is currently preoccupied with protecting children from abusive forms of touch. Touch can also feel less controllable for the carer than, say, the establishment of routines or the way food is 'done' in the home or unit.

Across three student studies that included residential staff members' views about touch, there was consensus amongst all research participants that touch was an appropriate and even important part of practice. Some participants made links between the importance of touch and attachment theory, and most made connections to relationships more generally.

In all three studies, staff members also expressed fears in relation to touching children, and many made references to risk. The most frequently cited risk was being the subject of an allegation (related to touch), but participants also talked about fears related to the (mis)perceptions of colleagues, touch escalating a child already in crisis and unclear organisational expectations. In two of the three studies, some staff members also spoke of their own poor experiences of touch or a lack of being touched when they were children. For some, these early childhood experiences motivated them to provide positive experiences of touch to their young charges; for others, it made it difficult for them to use touch in their practice.

It may be helpful to reflect on how much of what you're experiencing is to do with your own history related to touching and being touched, and how much of it might be what you're absorbing from the young person. If, for example, you have an uncharacteristic reaction to the way a young person touches you, then you may be absorbing something that is too uncontainable for him to bear (see Chapter Four). What you're feeling can help you to understand what the child is communicating to you through touch. Or, those feelings might be telling you something about yourself.

Because of the potential emotional charge, it's important that you get support in making sense of touch as it relates to how you care for children. This can happen in individual or group supervision or with your support worker. It can also happen more informally in discussions with fellow carers. Touch is a good topic of discussion for consultancy or training sessions. Also, you will have your own touch-related needs and these should not be ignored in your efforts to meet the needs of children you care for. Friends and family may be the most obvious source for meeting your needs.

How you and others can help

On the one hand, it's important to reflect on touch: the way it happens in your caring exchanges, what it means to you and what it might mean to the child, other children and the organisation you work in. It also might be good to consider how changing the way you incorporate touch into your care can increase the positive effect you have on a child and his development. Above all, touch should be considered within the context of your relationship with the child. For children too young to use language or who are affected by significant communication impairment, touch will likely be the most important medium for building relationships.

Pause for Reflection

Think about how touch happens in the everyday activities of providing care. How might the child you care for feel about this? How might he let you know? How do you feel about it? Are there missed opportunities for conveying care and respect through touch as opposed to it just being a task?

On the other hand, if touch is thought of as some sort of technique that is instrumentally applied, or if you become highly self-conscious and wooden in your physical interactions, it probably won't have a very positive outcome. Keeping touch as natural as possible while keeping in mind many of the considerations in this chapter may be quite challenging. Towards this end, it helps to strive for self-awareness as opposed to self-consciousness. Self-awareness is about tuning into what is going on with you and how that may be affecting the interaction. Self-consciousness is more about applying negative judgements to ourselves or assuming negative judgements from others. It has a worrying aspect.

Carers sometimes wonder about whether they should ask permission before touching a young person in their care. Sometimes, his non-verbal communication will let you know it's okay; other times, it's hard to tell. This is a good example of how challenging it can be to get a good balance of self-aware, thoughtful and natural. The answer is there's no easy formula and it will depend on the nature of your relationship with the young person. We would argue against a blanket approach that always involves asking permission, as it reduces spontaneity and in some cases may interfere with mutuality. There are other times, however, where it might be what a child needs in order to feel safe and respected. Being attuned to your child (see Chapter Three) will help you to know.

If in doubt, checking in with the child might serve a similar function but is less likely to send a message that touch is risky. A statement like, 'I'd really like to give you a hug right now, but I can't tell if you'd be okay with that' makes available to the young person what you are feeling and demonstrates an interest in what he is feeling. Sharing what touch means to you and checking out its meaning to a young person, especially related to a particular encounter, can also help to reduce mistaken assumptions or more general anxieties. For example, if a young person shrinks from your attempt to give him a hug, one response might be, 'I was just so happy to see you, I wanted to give you a cuddle. It looks like that was too full-on for you. You okay?' Often, young people won't always have the self-awareness to know what they're feeling, and they may not even be aware of their reaction to you. So it may be helpful to offer some possibilities to help the young person name their feelings if they appear to be struggling ('You got a fright there' or 'You didn't like me touching your head'). In this type of situation, the young person might have felt invaded, embarrassed or even just startled. Without checking in, it is easy to misunderstand the reaction.

A common approach to negotiating touch has become to ask the child, 'Would you like a hug?' While this approach shouldn't necessarily be rejected outright, it misses the opportunity to let the child in on what you're thinking and feeling (i.e. 'I want to hug you'). It also weakens one of the most important messages we convey to children through touch, and that has to do with their inherent lovability. The implicit messages we convey through touch are more powerful than when they're communicated simply through words. These messages include, 'you're not disgusting', 'you're not alone', 'you're lovable', 'I want to be connected with you' or 'I'm here for you'. For a child who hasn't consistently had these messages during his early years, it becomes even more imperative that he is regularly reassured of these things, and touch is an important vehicle for such communication.

There are so many different ways that touch happens within a home or unit. A student doing her PhD on touch in residential child care recently commented that she observed so much touching going on between the staff and the young people – much more than they are probably aware of and much of it initiated by the young people. If this is not the case in your own caring experience, it may be in a child's best interest to maximise opportunities for physical contact, but it must be tailored to the child's needs, the relationship you have with him and the circumstances of each particular interaction. Again, this requires tuning in.

Spotlight on Practice

John had a long history of numerous broken placements and frequent physical restraints. The residential team felt the pattern was being repeated with them. They were struggling to find ways to get him through situations involving serious, imminent harm without resorting to restraint, and it sometimes felt he was looking for close, physical contact in some of these situations. They were also worried that the placement may break down. They came to realise, based on some details of his history and their direct experience of him, that they needed to focus not just on what was happening when he was in crisis, but what was happening at other times too. One of the things they did was to initiate playful and affectionate touch with him much more often and when he was coping well. Sometimes these were obvious things, like ruffling his hair or locking arms when walking down the corridor. Other times it was more subtle, like sitting that bit closer on the couch. They started the increase tentatively, and when he responded favourably, they continued to deliberately increase their physical contact with him. They were amazed at how quickly the situations that had led to restraint seemed to just fizzle out, and the incidence of restraining him reduced to almost zero over the next several months. This wasn't the only part of their effort to break the pattern of physical restraint, but at the time and in retrospect, it felt like the most important part.

You might notice that when you attempt to increase the frequency of affectionate physical contact, the child or young person resists your attempts. Under these circumstances, your instinct might be to respect the child's implicit messages of 'don't touch me' and keep your physical distance. Yet consideration should be given to the other possible messages that might be conveyed here. The child might feel he is too unlovable, disgusting or simply 'bad' to receive warmth or affection, whether physically or otherwise. When this is the case, keeping your distance tells the child 'you're right!' This is a particularly tricky area of caring practice; the child will need to feel safe and respected, but also will need his underlying negative beliefs about himself to be gently but firmly challenged. Some of the checking in described above might be useful, as well as persistence and flexibility in the ways you continue to attempt contact. Ruth recalls a special moment with one boy who, after repeated rejections of her attempts to convey affection, closed his eyes and leaned back into her hand as she gently touched the back of his head. This was only possible after she tuned into his constant messages of 'I'm not worthy; I'm bad'. This awareness bolstered her determination not to unconsciously accept this view of him, but instead to reflect back to him her own fondness of him.

Another way you can help children who struggle with touch is to utilise opportunities to model physical contact in the home or unit. Again, this should be done in a self-aware (rather than self-conscious) way. Consider how adults and other members of the family or group touch one another and what messages this conveys about the physical dimension of relationships. Modelling the sexual dimension of a sexual relationship isn't possible, and even discussing such a personal part of oneself will be off limits for many. Yet some young people have had extremely distorted modelling of this very important aspect of life. Highlighting other examples, whether in film, books or television, may be one way of opening up conversations that help young people to explore their understandings of appropriate and inappropriate sexual touch.

Finally, certain animals can provide important bridging experiences of safe and rewarding physical contact; a relationship with a pet or horse can be extremely important to some children and can pave the way for more connected human relationships. Providing access and supporting a child to have a relationship with a pet can be another important way you can help.

Spotlight on Practice

Kurt, after being punched by Martin, is at a bit of a loss. He's aware that this might be Martin's way of telling him he's hurt or angry at him for being away, but he's not sure how to proceed. He doesn't really feel like giving him a cuddle anymore, and he realises he's a bit angry himself. He could respond by playfully punching him back, but given his own anger and Martin's history, this could well escalate. Even if it doesn't, is this the best way to deal with Martin's hurt and anger? Yet if he simply disengages, that will probably compound

Martin's already existing feelings of rejection or abandonment. He decides to sit alongside Martin on the settee and playfully lean into him a little bit to see where it goes from there.

Everyday things you might like to try

- For children who resist being touched, *experiment with playful or fleeting touch* that conveys affection and respect but doesn't draw too much attention to the encounter.

  ○ If the child flinches or lets you know in some other way he wasn't okay with being touched, acknowledge this. For example, you may just say 'I can see you didn't like me touching your head'.

  ○ Invite the child to engage in simple, non-threatening games that involve touch like 'one potato' or 'thumb wars'.

- For a child who is excessive in the amount of touch he initiates, *experiment with other ways of communicating your attention*, affection and ability to keep him safe. This might include spoken messages, shared activities and simple acts of nurture, like a cup of tea.

  ○ Gently let him know how the excessive touch feels and offer an alternative, for example, 'It's not comfortable you sitting on my lap, but you could sit here next to me.'

- Try *indirect touch*. In younger children this can be done by cuddling or patting toys. In older children, pets can provide a bridging experience to more comfort with human touch. As you are saying soothing words you can use soothing actions.

- Consider a *massage therapist*, for your child or for you. Where appropriate, incorporate hand, foot, head or back massages into your caring practices.

- Sometimes children will offer you opportunities to touch them through *other means* – putting on a plaster, dyeing their hair, buttoning a shirt, face painting or applying fake tattoos. All of these allow the slow beginnings of touch. It is useful to keep your eyes open for these times.

- *Pamper nights* can be another fun way to increase positive experiences of touch. These can include hand and foot massage and nail painting, face masks, aromatherapy and nice food. In our experience children and young people (and most of them are girls!) love this kind of thing. Don't be afraid to join in and pamper yourself a bit too.

- *Physical contact through sport* can also be a safe way to feel physically connected. Make the most of opportunities for pats on the back, high fives and group huddles.

Conclusion

All human beings need touch; in the case of children, the forms, frequency and intensity that they need will depend on their developmental levels and whether reparative experiences are necessary. This should be your starting point in thinking about the place of physical contact in your care practices. While you may not always be sure, it is better to proceed with warmth and sensitivity than avoid touch completely.

Further reading and resources

Booth, P.B. and Jernberg, A.M. (2010) *Theraplay: Helping Parents and Children Build Better Relationships through Attachment Based Play*. San Francisco, CA: Jossey-Bass.

Field, T. (2014) *Touch*, Second edition. Cambridge, MA: The MIT Press.

Steckley, L. (2009) 'Don't Touch.' *CYC-Online* (December 2009). Available at: www.cyc-net.org/cyc-online/cyconline-dec2009-steckley.html (accessed 12 August 2015).

Steckley, L. (2010) 'Touching Thoughts: Parts 1 & 2.' *CYC-Online* (March and May 2010). Available at: http://cyc-net.org/cyc-online/cyconline-mar2010-steckley.html and http://cyc-net.org/cyc-online/cyconline-may2010-steckley.html (accessed 12 August 2015).

The Touch Research Institute. For information and research about touch go to The Touch Research Institute. Available at: www6.miami.edu/touch-research

9

Communicating

Introduction

There is a vast literature on how human beings communicate, but the majority share a view that we 'talk' and 'listen' using much more than spoken words. People are in constant dialogue with themselves and with the world around them. We are sending signals using both our conscious and unconscious minds. In fact, communication is such a taken-for-granted part of our daily lives that we only really pay it any attention when it goes wrong.

This chapter is a chance for us to stop and think about how we communicate with the children we look after; what it is we are telling our children with our words and deeds; where these messages might be coming from; and how they might be being received. The chapter is underpinned by the assumption that adults talk *with* children not *to* them and that, in turn, children have a lot to say that we, as adults, need to pay attention to.

It is hoped that the chapter will answer the following questions:

- Where do we learn the rules of communication?

- Why is being aware of communication important for residential workers and foster carers?

- How do I listen not only to what my child says but also what she does?

The importance of communication: I sound just like my mother

The ways in which we communicate with others are endless. Those who know us well will be able to 'read' our every move. It is not simply the words that we use, but the gestures, tones and rhythms that accompany these words which, taken together, produce meaning. The tone of our voice, the rhythm of our speech, what we are doing with our face, our eyes and our body all tell the world around us something about our inner state, what we are thinking and feeling. Unsurprisingly, most of this happens without us even knowing it. In relation to communication, we are so programmed by our early experiences that it is usually only in exceptional circumstances that we become aware not just of *what*, but *how* we are communicating.

Pause for Reflection

Think about the last time you planned what you were going to say. Did you include non-verbal communication in your planning?

In answering the question above, it is likely that you will have picked a job interview or formal meeting as your example of 'conscious communication'. Or you may have picked an experience of discussing a thorny relationship issue. What these types of activities have in common is a desire not only to be heard and understood, but also to be seen in a particular light. This link between communication and personhood, in other words what we say shaping how we see ourselves and hope others will see us, is a key aspect of communication.

Normally, most of us communicate from an unconscious place. Our sense of who we are, or how we want to be seen, takes an unconscious back seat but is never far away! Unconsciously driven communication makes sense. How could we get through the day if we had to carefully consider and choose every movement, word, gesture or facial expression? However, as foster carers and residential staff, we need to be more aware than others about how and what we are communicating and whether or not we are being understood by those we care for. In order to do this, we need to think about where our style and patterns of communication come from. In a sense this can be thought of as our communication programming – how we have been programmed to talk, listen, use gestures, pitch our voice and hold our bodies.

The most powerful communication programming comes from the everyday communications that we experience in childhood, primarily those delivered by and shared with our immediate family. Such family communication teaches us ways to let someone know what our needs are, our thoughts and our feelings. Family communication may have shown us ways to deepen relationships, to manage conflict and disagreement as well as demonstrate tenderness and intimacy. These patterns can almost be thought of as our family language. They tell us not only how to talk and communicate, but also what information we are permitted to tell others and what should be hidden or kept to ourselves.

Pause for Reflection

Think back to when you were living in your childhood home. How did your parents let others in the family know when they were tired or hungry? How did they let others know about their successes? How did they let others know they were angry or that they were loved by them?

These ways of expressing ourselves are powerful imprints and establish a rule book for communication that we take with us into other relationships, both within and outside family life. These rules relate to *how* to communicate as well as *what* is allowed to be communicated, by whom, when and where.

What you might notice

As you can imagine having read this far, how we communicate with children is heavily influenced by how we have been taught to both communicate with and view children. In caring for looked-after children, we need to give our unconscious communication more attention. Whilst our own families might well know and understand us, the children who have entered our homes or residential units will not. This is not only because they are new to our family, but also because they may have had a different experience of how communication 'works'.

Many of the children who we look after have learned to pay exceptionally close attention to what adults are saying with their voices, faces and bodies. They may have had to anticipate crisis, violence, absence or attack. Tiny changes in our face or voice will be noticed and interpreted through the 'programming' that the children have had in communication. Sometimes this can interfere with their ability to take in our words.

Pause for Reflection

What do you know about how your child was talked to within the family home? Was she in a situation where moods, actions or feelings could change rapidly and unpredictably?

At the very least, the children you are looking after will have come through a major separation from their birth family to come into your care. They will have had to listen to information communicated by a variety of adults, in a range of ways. Often adults forget that children hear and feel so much of what is going on around them. This is regardless of age or disability. This will have played a part in how the child relates to you and the extent to which she is able to really hear what it is that you are saying. Often, the children we look after will be mistrustful of statements about security, terms of affection or encouragement to trust. You might also notice your child using language, terms or phrases that include social work 'jargon' (which is not always clearly understood) or that suggest a level of connection with you, or depth of relationship, that seems surprising.

What you might feel

Communication can be a confusing and frustrating process within any relationship. However, living with children who have had experiences of not being listened to or who have known adults to dismiss or silence their voices can increase these feelings. Sometimes, straightforward statements or questions can be met with blank expressions, vague responses or angry and rejecting words. It is worth thinking about whether these reactions are part of exploring and testing the relationship, the rules of relationships or the stage of development. However, it may also be because what we have said is not clear or is open to interpretations. Talking straight and talking simply is often the most effective way of communicating until we can gain a clearer understanding of how our child has experienced communication in the past. For example, one child who Ruth worked with responded angrily when she was told that she wouldn't see Ruth the next week for her usual session as Ruth had to go to a meeting. It was only after a lot of reflection and, later, wondering out loud with the child that it became clear that she had understood this statement to mean that there was a meeting arranged to talk about her of which she had no knowledge and to which she was not invited. Ruth was seen as having tricked her, lied to her and was going to be taking their work together and sharing it with others. It was a powerful reminder of what the spaces that we leave out can come to mean for children and how important it is to think through how key information will be heard.

Deep communication with children can also leave carers feeling incredibly lucky, profoundly moved or strongly connected. The moments where we have a chance to listen with our whole selves to the day our child has had, the experiences she has had or the feelings she has shared can be one of the best aspects of being involved in the care of children. Communication like this often appears to be very everyday, but for you and your child to have these moments together, moments when you are really talking and listening, can be healing. Not only can this help to heal past hurts, but it can repair more recent bumps in the relationship and serve to strengthen it further.

There are some residential units and indeed foster families where communication is placed at centre stage. The best ways to communicate with each individual child are identified, practised, reviewed and adapted by all who are involved in the child's care. Staff and carers report feeling much more confident in their caregiving and describe a sense of knowing the child more deeply. Historically, services set up for children with disabilities or who have recognised communication difficulties appear to be much more forward thinking than many of the rest of us. However, we can learn a lot from these approaches regardless of whether or not our child has a recognised disability. One of the most exciting approaches to this is the creation of a **Total Communication Environment** (we've included some reading on this at the end) where all forms of communication (sensory, visual, spoken, symbolic) are recognised and used.

Communication also extends to how information is shared and exchanged with people outside your home. A range of professionals, other family members, fellow workers or carers (the list is endless) and how they communicate with you, and you with them, can have a significant impact on how you feel. Foster carers and residential workers who we have learned from over the years have described a range of experiences relating to 'professional' communication as well as communication with friends and family. For some, there has been a sense of being heard and understood in relation to the experiences of having the role of 'carer'. For others, there have been feelings of fear around the sharing of feelings, views or experiences with others. You may have had times where you have felt that to talk about what you really feel or think will call into question your ability to remain in your role or that you will be thought of in a negative way. You may worry about where the information that you give about yourself will go and how it will be shared with others. There may be times where you feel confused or shut out of decisions being made about your child or unclear about what is being expected of you. The impact of these feelings is explored in more detail in Chapter Four.

How you and others can help

Children's chronological age will play a part in how they experience communication. Having some knowledge of these 'norms of development' is useful in considering how best to let children know information or how to ask them questions (we must also keep in mind how trauma and disability can impact on this). For example, it is not until the age of 6 that children have an established understanding of time; therefore, questions about *when* can be difficult up to that point. Similarly, it is not until around the age of 8 that children develop enough abstract reasoning to answer *why* something occurred. Children's communication skills grow in sophistication as they age. However, it is also important to consider not only a child's chronological age but also the conditions she has experienced which may have supported her development, or where aspects of development may have been compromised by trauma, neglect or disability.

Crucial in the development of communication is the development of a language for feelings. Children are not born knowing what to call the changes that they experience in their bodies, minds and hearts; rather, it is through their interactions with their primary caregiver that words are given and then later, shared and told. Many of the children we care for have not had these crucial experiences. They have not had an adult consistently noticing, naming and accepting the feelings that they have.

The concept of 'feelings' covers so many complex and nuanced emotions that children need a great deal of help to be able to give voice to them. Without a name for the feeling, the ways to identify, express and ultimately get rid of the feelings are reduced. Instead children may say that they are 'bored', 'tired', 'FINE!', or show and expel feelings by slamming doors, shouting or, perhaps most challenging, closing down.

A responsive and attuned parent begins to know and experience the child's feeling. As discussed in Chapter Four, the parent names and holds the feeling for the child and in so doing, gives it back to the child in a much more manageable way. This is also known as **co-regulation**. What an amazing thing this is; it is so important to children's development and recovery from trauma.

Caring for someone who hasn't been brought up with the same communication programming places greater responsibility on the adult to be aware of his or her own, as well as the child's, verbal and non-verbal communication. Crucially, the adult needs to be able to 'read' the child and this takes time, acceptance, curiosity and pace. Allowing children to lead communication can feel unusual for adults. It is usually us who tell children what to do, when and how to do it. By letting children take the lead we can begin to know and understand what matters to the child and also send a message to the child that we are interested in her as an individual.

Hilary Kennedy, an educational psychologist (whose book is included in the 'Further reading and resources' section), suggests that, where possible, adults start interactions with children based on what the child has initiated through their words or behaviours. In other words, we start with what we see instead of starting conversations with a question. Typically, this involves naming the behaviour, followed by naming the feeling and then thinking together about future action. This might look like the following:

1. You're busy there on the computer (*name the behaviour*)

2. You're frustrated that we have to stop and have tea (*name the feeling*)

3. What can we do to make sure that we get to eat together? (*future action*)

This approach to communication allows the child to have more power and control over the interaction. It may not be possible to approach all interactions with your child in this way, but at times where you think your child might struggle with your instruction, power dynamic or challenge, this model offers a way of getting alongside the child and showing a degree of acceptance for the feelings that your actions may engender. This is crucial for children who might very quickly fall into a sense of shame or may experience adult instructions as a precursor for attack.

As adults, our normal interactions with children often take on a variety of purposes rooted in the role that we have (or think we have) in relation to them. Adults can feel pressure to instruct, correct, teach or guide a child's thoughts, actions and beliefs. However, what we know from research is that for this to work, children need to trust us and to feel safe enough to be in a position to learn.

Spotlight on Practice

Ruth opened the door of her workplace to a 9-year-old girl, Sara. Sara announced that she had fallen and that her leg was broken. Her carer, standing behind her told Ruth, 'She's totally fine, she just slipped'. Here the carer was taking the role of guidance and instructor, sending the implicit messages: 'You shouldn't tell lies. You are fine. Stop making a fuss. Behave for therapy.'

Once in the playroom Sara continued to repeat that her leg was broken. Ruth decided to go with what she was presenting. The conversation went as follows:

Ruth: It is broken.

Sarah: It's snapped in half.

Ruth: You are hanging on to your broken leg there.

Sara: Yes, it's so sore. I've got to keep it together like this (Sara holds her leg with two hands).

Ruth: It's just falling apart and it's really painful.

Sara: It's agony.

Ruth: You want me to know that it's agony. Do you need a bandage?

Sara: Yes, well maybe just a plaster. (Ruth gets a plaster and helps Sara to put it on.)

Sara: I think it's a bit better now.

Ruth: You were in a lot of pain and now it feels a wee bit better. I needed to look after you.

Sara: I have a lot of sore bits.

Ruth: You're sore all over.

By attending to what Sara brought to the session, Ruth was able to accept what she was saying, allowing her to initiate the interaction. Rather than correct Sara's reality, Ruth stayed with the underlying message that Sara was bringing ('I need you to attend to me'). It may be that Sara wanted to communicate a deeper sense of pain, which would make sense given that she had had a difficult visit with her birth parents a few days before. Either way, by having the need noticed and attended to, Sara was able to relax and feel that she had been heard and understood.

This type of communication can be difficult for carers to manage. It can seem like children are 'taking us for a ride'. Indeed, sometimes that may be what is happening, in which case that too needs to be noticed, attended to and understood: 'It's hard to trust adults and you're not sure if I am any different.'

Sara's example also reminds us that communication often occurs through what sociologists refer to as 'symbols'. In Chapter Seven, we talked about this in a bit more detail but in brief, symbolic communication occurs when something is used to stand for, or represent, a deeper message that the individual needs to communicate. Like many forms of communication, this is likely to be an unconscious process.

Children often communicate through another object. It could be a toy, food or even an imaginary friend. It's easier for carers when these 'third objects' have a voice (e.g. 'Teddy doesn't like the dark') because then the adult can respond verbally ('It's important that I know Teddy doesn't like the dark. What do you think would make Teddy feel better?'). More challenging is when we don't realise that our child is trying to talk to us symbolically. What at first might appear strange or challenging behaviour is often a means through which a child is trying to let us know something about her needs or feelings.

Spotlight on Practice

One boy, David, that Ruth looked after in residential care liked to tell her things about her car. He would get books from the library and when she was on shift, would want to check tyre pressure, oil levels and other mechanical operations. It took a while to work out what it was that David was trying to say in this behaviour. Ruth didn't know it at the time, but what she did was what Janet West (1996), a writer on play therapy, refers to as 'levels of reflection' (we've included her book in the 'Further reading and resources' section).

Stage One

First, Ruth reflected what she saw and experienced: 'You're really interested in my car.' And then later, 'You want to make sure my car works well.' Because David's interest in the car didn't seem to be going away, Ruth felt that she wasn't getting at what it was that David was communicating to her through the car.

Stage Two

In supervision, Ruth took apart what was happening – David was interested in the car; David wanted to have knowledge about the car; David wanted to use the knowledge to check the car was working; David wanted Ruth to know that he was checking the car. Eventually, Ruth began to wonder whether David was trying to let her know something much deeper and was using the car symbolically. In supervision, they wondered together whether maybe David wanted to check that Ruth was safe and that she was going to get to him every day. Once she had begun to make these connections, she started to use West's next level of reflection. At the next natural opportunity, Ruth observed to David, 'Sometimes children can really worry that cars break down.' This seemed to resonate with David and he agreed that 'cars can be trouble'.

Stage Three

Next Ruth took it a stage further. She mused aloud, 'I guess if cars break down kids might worry that their adult won't get to see them or might get hurt.'

David said nothing but stopped in his tracks for a while, almost as if his conscious thoughts were beginning to form from something that may well have been deeply unconscious. He then said 'No! You're wrong'.

Stage Four

Finally, after a good few months of car checks, Ruth tried the higher level reflection: 'I wonder if you ever worry that something will happen to me and I won't be able to look after you any more.' David was able to think about this and began to talk about his worry that Ruth would leave and that no one else would know what had happened to him when he had lived with his birth family.

Whilst this communication took place over an extensive period, Ruth stuck with what David was doing, what she was seeing and feeling, and then slowly, she began to share that with him. What was important was that she recognised that the car, and the behaviours around the car, were providing David with a symbolic means of exploring and expressing something that was just too hard to do.

You don't necessarily need to know about levels of reflection or use the exact approach illustrated above, but what it shows is the importance of children setting the pace and adults recognising the symbol or metaphor and working with that rather than shutting it down. It also demonstrates how much children can persevere to get the communication over to another person.

Being aware of how you communicate with your child and planning how you might respond to what she is telling you verbally and non-verbally can feel strange and uncomfortable. Using reflection rather than answering questions, staying with the child's view of the world rather than immediately correcting her and naming the feeling that the child may be sharing with you all need practice. Carers and staff have reported feeling a range of emotions whilst undertaking these aspects of communication.

Feelings have ranged from silly, embarrassed, false, to deeper questions about who they are by using these approaches, including 'I sound like a therapist', 'I sound weird', 'I sound American'.

There are no hard and fast rules, but what is important is that communication is reflected on and, where possible, planned and considered. These types of communication can feel a bit clunky and false when you first start to use them, but what you will quickly find is that they serve to open up, rather than close down communication. They also show a child that you are listening not just to their words but also to their whole self. For many children this will be a first and may feel quite unsettling. However, following a child's lead can take you to the most wonderful places. As an adult, it also frees you from the roles of 'fixer', interrogator and controller that many children will want to put you in.

By listening and responding reflectively, we start to model a different way of communicating that relies less on power and control and much more on empathy, honesty and openness. Talking with children as you yourself would want to be talked to is crucial to this. So often we have heard parents shouting at children 'stop shouting' or telling them snarlingly 'don't talk to me like that'. It can take a while, but modelling the style of communication that you hope children will develop is vital.

Communication, talking with rather than at children, takes us right back to the dance of attunement that we mentioned in Chapter Three. Often the rhythm of the dance that we establish with children can be far from the one that we set out to achieve. By letting children take the initiative and accepting and attending to them, we slow the beat down and begin to dance *together* rather than being tied in a jarring struggle for power over who has control over the beat.

Letting the child take the initiative is not the same as letting the child take full control. There may well be times when we have to remind the child of the boundaries of behaviour and ways of communicating that are hurtful or which will turn people away. How we do this is to model something very powerful about how words and non-verbal communication can be strong but accepting. Often the best way to do this is to start with what you see: 'You're really angry that I've said no, but I am not for shouting at. You can shout at the cushion in your bedroom.' Gary Landreth (2002), a play therapist whose book is included in the 'Further reading and resources' section, stresses the importance of accepting and acknowledging the child's feeling, setting her a limit but providing her with an outlet for the feeling rather than shutting it off (see Chapter Ten for more on this). Teaching children to manage and express feelings in this way is strongly reinforced by what we model for them. For example, we may say, 'I'm so mad at that traffic warden I need to take three big breaths.'

Linked to this is the willingness on the part of the adults to own up to mistakes in communication. Going to a child and apologising for not listening properly or for jumping to conclusions or raising your voice is the best way to show her how to acknowledge, apologise and repair a relationship when communication has gone wrong. It is never a sign of weakness in an adult to do this. It shows children that you are strong and trusting and that you respect them and yourself.

Everyday things you might like to try

- Think about your evening with the child last night. Jot down some of the different ways she was communicating with you and you with them. Were those communications successful? Did you both get what you needed from these? What do you notice now? What would you do differently next time?

- Practise reflection and naming both directly relating to the child's own feelings and more generally (this can be easier for some children to tolerate): 'You're angry'; 'Sometimes kids can feel really fed up when adults don't get what they are trying to say.' It's as important to say what you see in positive situations, not just when things are bad. For example: 'You were so happy to get in that pool today.' Think about your tone and facial expressions and see if anyone would be willing to let you practise with them.

- Focus on a *repeated behaviour that is puzzling you*, but seems to be communicating something. With your supervisor or mentor make a plan for how you might use the 'levels of reflection' described earlier in this chapter to discuss the meaning behind this behaviour with the child. Think together about all the different things the child might be trying to tell you and write them down. Go through each one. How might you want to respond to each underlying communication? Remember these might not be in the child's own awareness.

- Experiment with ways of *enhancing your non-verbal communication* with the child. Think about things you can do to communicate 'you are safe and you are precious to me' without using words. Things you could do might include: increasing the amount of nurturing touch you provide (see Chapter Eight for more ideas about touch), providing special food or drinks and certain times to show care and provide comfort (see Chapter Seven for more ideas about food), spending more quality time with the child (see Chapter Three for more ideas about developing relationships) or using symbols, play, pictures, music or art.

- Experiment with drawing up a 'communications policy'. This doesn't have to be a formal document but rather a way of mapping what types of communication you want to promote as well as the best ways or approaches you have found to connect with your child.

- Often as adults we can get caught up in spoken words. *Try to think about ways of interacting with your child that don't rely on language.* Ways of being together and sharing a connection are often best done with limited talk. You might want to try simple games like blowing a cotton wool ball along the ground or table, going back and forth, trying to see how many times you can do it together. Singing together or making music can also be a way to communicate in a way that is safe and shared. This doesn't have to be too formal or planned. The best times are often the ones where we spontaneously find connections with each other.

- Playing hide and seek can allow lots of quiet space but also anticipation, discovery and reveal. To feel as if you are someone worth finding and to experience being the source of joy at discovery is such a profound, and often missing, aspect of our children's experiences.

Conclusion

The topic of 'communication' is vast. This chapter has focused on the importance of thinking carefully about how we communicate with the children we care for and on encouraging your freedom to reflect, on your own or in supervision, about why you communicate and respond in the way that you do. Often the children that you care for have lived with adults whose communication involved confusion, deception, threat, avoidance, dismissiveness or rejection. They bring this model of communication with them and therefore a fundamental task of the caregiver is to offer alternative ways to be with other people, to let others know inner thoughts and feelings, and to communicate needs and wants. This is no easy task and will rely on you feeling safe and supported within your support relationships. You may have to look at or change what you do and say. You may have to alter your communication style for each of the children that you care for in order to best meet their needs. Our job is often, as Fahlberg would say, to 'decode children's signals'. If we can notice, name and hold onto what these signals are, we are much more able to help them find other, more successful ways of sending their message to the world.

Further reading and resources

Landreth, G. (2002) *Play Therapy: The Art of the Relationship.* Hove: Brunner-Routledge.

Tait, A. and Wosu, H. (2013) *Direct Work with Vulnerable Children: Playful Activities and Strategies for Communication.* London: Jessica Kingsley Publishers.

West, J. (1996) *Child Centred Play Therapy.* London: Hodder Education.

Wilson, C. (2013) 'A different language: Implementing the total communication approach.' *Scottish Journal of Residential Child Care 12,* 1, 34–45.

10

Working with
Pain-based Behaviour

Introduction

At some point or another, in all of our relationships, we can expect to encounter behaviour that we find difficult to deal with. In relation to caring for children and young people, this is often referred to as 'challenging behaviour'. Working with challenging behaviour can be the most difficult part of our caring work, and it often brings up uncomfortable and undesirable feelings in us. This chapter will focus on some of the difficult behaviours you may encounter in your caring work and how you might respond to them. It will offer ways of thinking about behaviour that may help with related difficult feelings and, in turn, increase the effectiveness of your responses.

We will also spend some time exploring and acknowledging just how very upsetting, demanding and potentially threatening, both physically and emotionally, some of these behaviours can be. Dealing with these behaviours is the thing that most carers find most difficult about the job they do. For some of you reading this book, you may also be dealing with the physical and emotional scars of these behaviours. If this is the case, it is important that your hurts and humiliations are acknowledged and you are supported to heal and move on. In this chapter we will provide some suggestions for how you might do this.

In discussing challenging or difficult behaviour, this chapter will address related questions that carers typically have, including:

- How can my everyday interactions with a child be healing when it feels like our interactions, every day, are a battle?

- How do I keep boundaries and set limits in a way that isn't punitive, especially with a child who regularly or severely pushes or breaks them?

- What do I do when I've tried everything and nothing seems to work?

The importance of how we think and talk about behaviour

The way we think about behaviour and what is sometimes defined as misbehaviour affects how we respond to it, how effective our response is, and whether a child or young person benefits from our efforts. Behaviour is often referred to as a form of communication or an expression of need. For children with communication difficulties, behaviours which we may find challenging are often the only way they convey to us that things aren't okay.

We have chosen to call this chapter, 'Working with Pain-based Behaviour' (rather than the standard 'Working with Challenging Behaviour') because the behaviours we struggle with in our caring endeavours tend to come from a place of emotional (and sometimes, physical) pain. Jim Anglin, a former child and youth care worker who now teaches and does research in the field, coined the term *pain-based behaviour* in order to emphasise the deep and often longstanding pain that fuels 'challenging behaviour'.

Pause for Reflection

Think about a child you are caring for. Are there any behaviours that you find challenging? What do you think you child is telling you with her behaviour? What feeling(s) do you think is/are being shown to you?

Much as we might try to separate the behaviour from the child, children often become labelled as 'difficult' or 'challenging' and there is a danger that when they become defined as such, their other, more positive behaviours and qualities are not noticed or reflected back to them. The use of the term 'pain-based behaviour' helps us to hold in mind the child – a child who is in pain – and not just her behaviour. It also helps to remind us that exposure to pain-based behaviour can trigger painful feelings in us, whether as a result of absorption (as discussed in Chapter Four) or our own buttons getting pressed.

Importance of our selves

A shift in focus from the child's behaviour to our own feelings and behaviour may be one key to improving relationships. When we refer to behaviour as difficult or challenging, we are almost always referring to someone else's behaviour. We often assume that a particular behaviour is difficult and challenging for everyone else too. Yet different people find different behaviours difficult. In addition, some behaviour might bother the same person at one point in her life, but not at another. Rarely do we refer to our own behaviour as challenging, and yet there will indeed be people who find at least some of our behaviours challenging; upon reflection, we are also likely to be uncomfortably challenged by our own behaviours sometimes. For example, Laura finds her own tendency to procrastinate a challenge – not just in terms of overcoming the bad habit, but in terms of the impact it sometimes has on her.

Put simply, the most important behaviour we must work with is our own. When faced with an angry, aggressive young person it is easy to lose sight of this. This means more than just resisting the urge to retaliate, though that in itself can be difficult. It takes good supervision, support and advice as well as knowledge and skills to hold onto an awareness of ourselves and act usefully on that awareness right there in the moment, even just under normal conditions; doing so when faced with the pain-based behaviour of a young person or group can sometimes feel impossible.

How you make sense of behaviour – whether you see it as designed to hurt or anger you, or whether you see it as an expression of need or pain – will have a big impact on how you feel about and react to it. In addition, tuning into how the young person is making sense of her own and your actions can help you to keep yourself in a place of helpfulness. Each of you may be making very different meanings about what is going on, and sometimes this in itself can be the source of conflict. Thom Garfat, a former Child and Youth Care Worker who now writes books and articles for carers, found in his study that meaning-making was a key ingredient for carers' interventions to be effective.

As we become attuned to how young people make sense of their world and specific events in it, we will be more effective in working with them in a way that better helps them to manage their own behaviour. For this to be possible, we must also be aware of how we make meaning of situations and events, consistently striving to keep in mind that any interpretation is merely *our own* meaning made about a situation or event. A good place to start is by looking at how our own misbehaviour was understood and responded to when we were children. It's a good idea to cultivate a habit of wondering about how similar or different each young person's experiences have been to your own, and how potential differences might impart very different meanings about how you respond to certain behaviours. For instance, your efforts to address a young person's swearing may be experienced by that young person as you trying to change her into someone who will no longer fit into her family or community.

Pause for Reflection

Think about the last time you had to respond to challenging behaviour. What happened? What thoughts did you have at the time? What emotions were you feeling? What did you say? What did you communicate to the child using body language, facial expressions and tone of voice? What might you do differently in the future to respond to this behaviour?

Limits and boundaries, shame and guilt

Within all of this discussion about understanding behaviour, what it communicates, the pain that underlies it and our own reactions to it, it could be easy to overlook the importance of boundaries and limits. An environment where there are no interpersonal boundaries or limits on behaviour is not going to enable children and young people to feel safe or internalise a sense of respect for others.

It will be challenging to maintain boundaries and set limits without at least some children or young people in your care experiencing this as punishment. Yet we know that punishment is ineffective in promoting the development of internal controls or respect for others. Punishment also tends to damage relationships.

There may even be times when it feels like punishment is the appropriate response. There can be something unsettling about a young person who doesn't appear to feel any guilt for hurtful or destructive behaviour. You may feel that you need to make the child feel a sense of shame for what she has done. Guilt and shame are related, but they are actually very different experiences. Feelings of shame are focused on the self; they include humiliation and a sense of worthlessness. Guilt, on the other hand, is associated with a sense of empathy for others and regret or discomfort about something we have done.

Developmentally, feelings of shame come much earlier than feelings of guilt. Infants will experience shame from even mild reprimands, and this is very much a part of the process of learning not to do things that are hurtful or otherwise socially unacceptable. It's also painful to be flooded with feelings of humiliation and worthlessness.

For the experience of shame not to be damaging, an infant or toddler must experience a re-establishing of harmony in the relationship very quickly after admonishment. Often, parents or carers do this naturally by explaining why the child must not engage in the behaviour (e.g. because she could be hurt or could hurt others) and by reassuring the child of their love for her.

Children and young people who consistently did not experience a re-establishing of the relationship during infancy and toddlerhood will struggle to manage feelings of shame. They will have what has been referred to as **pervasive shame**. Pervasive shame is characterised by a sense of being worthless, blameworthy and bad. This is not only damaging to self-esteem and confidence, it engenders hopelessness and helplessness about being able to repair mistakes. Pervasive shame threatens psychological survival and must be defended against. A common defence for many children and young people is to cover the painful feelings with anger and aggression. The sense of power derived from angry feelings and behaviour can be much more manageable than the devastating effect of pervasive shame. The masking of shame is almost always unconscious and, over time, the shift to anger will be so fast that a child will be completely unaware of the underlying sense of shame. It's just too intolerable. If you have been caring for looked-after children for any significant time, then this will likely be very recognisable.

While this way of coping enables a child to survive pervasive shame, it interferes with or completely obstructs the development of empathy, the capacity to tolerate guilt and the development of a conscience. Under these circumstances, attempts to provoke a sense of guilt will often completely backfire. They will only reinforce the child's underlying sense of worthlessness, powerlessness and badness. They will also require her to fortify her anger and aggression to keep those feelings at bay, giving more cause for others to want her to feel guilty. It's easy to see how a vicious cycle can be perpetuated. Ways of managing boundaries and setting limits that are less likely to backfire will be discussed in the 'How you and others can help' section.

What you may notice

Most pain-based behaviour is hard to ignore, especially if it pushes your buttons. In this section, we will discuss some of the more common behaviours that carers tend to experiences as challenging, and we will encourage reflection about what those behaviours communicate, including the pain that underlies them.

Aggression is regarded by many carers as the most challenging behaviour that they have had to respond to. This can take many forms, including overt anger and destructiveness. Children may destroy property or physically hit you or turn their aggression towards themselves, hitting walls or banging their head against the floor. It can also manifest in more subtle expressions of hostility or defiance. This latter, more subtle behaviour is often referred to as **passive aggression**, and can include being secretive, stubborn or sulky. If subtle enough, passive aggression can escape your direct identification until later, when you're trying to figure out why you feel angry or uncomfortable about something that happened. As mentioned in the previous section, anger and aggression often cover up much more painful feelings of worthlessness and badness. They can also reflect a deeper sense of violation or feelings of being out of control. Passive-aggressive behaviour may also mask similar feelings, but it may also indicate an unconscious belief that anger is unacceptable or will lead to rejection. The strategy for some children may be to remain in a position of mild rejection so as not to risk the pain of being rejected by you.

Some children cope with shame and other painful emotions by withdrawing into themselves. They may have learned that adults cannot be relied upon and that the best defence is to rely upon themselves. They may also be 'shut down' or emotionally frozen due to previous trauma. Some children and young people who are withdrawn into themselves may use self-harm to cope. There are many different ways a child might harm herself, with common forms including cutting, scratching and hitting. In a study that explored how and why young people harm themselves, the Scottish Association for Mental Health (n.d.) found that the release of painful or difficult emotions (often in a way that didn't hurt others) was the most frequent reason that young people gave for harming themselves (the details of the study are in the 'Further reading and resources' section at the end). Self-punishment and the expression of self-hatred were some of the painful or difficult emotions that young people identified, and these are the kinds of feelings associated with pervasive shame. In addition, the need to break out of a sense of numbness and disconnection was another frequent reason the study participants gave for self-harm, and this points to the likelihood of previous trauma. Less than 10 per cent of the study participants indicated that they used self-harming behaviours in order to 'get care', and most experts agree that it is inaccurate and unhelpful to see self-harm as merely seeking attention. One research participant offers a much more insightful understanding:

> *I'm not manipulating you, or trying to scare you, I'm simply trying to reach out to you to tell you that I'm not okay. I'm in pain…I'm hurting on the inside, it's just easier to see on the outside. (Scottish Association for Mental Health n.d., p.11)*

Carers may also find it challenging to respond helpfully to children and young people's sexual behaviours. Some behaviours resulting from sexual play or curiosity are developmentally appropriate and it is important not to automatically assume that they reflect a deeper problem. You might find Toni Cavanagh-Johnson's booklet on sexual development (Cavanagh-Johnson 2005), listed in the 'Further reading' section at the end of this chapter, helpful in looking at what sexual behaviours can be expected at each developmental stage. According to HandsOnScotland, a large majority of children have engaged in some form of sexual behaviour by the time they reach 13 years old, and the vast majority of children's sexual behaviour is healthy. Some sexual behaviour, however, may well be cause for concern, including sexual acts that involve force, coercion, harm or a significant difference in age or power. Frequency and difficulty of redirection away from sexualised behaviours are other factors that may point to more serious underlying issues. Sexually problematic behaviour may be related to experiences of sexual interference or abuse, but not always. It may also reflect other traumatic experiences. In some children, such behaviour may be an unconscious way of letting you know about things that have happened in the past and their related confusion, worry or shame. Some young people may express their feelings of worthlessness through excessively promiscuous behaviour, while others may use sexual interactions to feel in control.

As children grow and develop, their social worlds become increasingly important and they will likely exercise a growing need for greater independence. This can be especially challenging when their sense of personal responsibility does not grow apace, and this can be a normal state of affairs for typically developing young people who have not experienced significant adversity. It can be even more frustrating or concerning with young people whose adversities have interfered with a strong sense of self-worth and personal responsibility. This can be especially tricky when a young person is keen to spend time with people who give you cause for concern. The prevalence of social media as a way of meeting and connecting with others has complicated things further. In many respects, we know less about and have less control over the choices of the young people we care for as a result. If the chosen relationships are especially damaging to the young person, it may reflect an underlying sense of worthlessness. However, it may be hard for the young person to see this. Further conflict, especially if experienced as rejection, can often make things worse.

There is no easy formula (or even difficult formula) for getting it right with any of these pain-based behaviours, though we will offer some strategies in the 'How you and others can help' section later in this chapter. Developing and maintaining curiosity about what the behaviour is communicating is a good starting point, and you may begin to notice patterns that help you to understand better. Particular kinds of situations, circumstances or even sensory stimulation may be a trigger for a child. Smells, for example, can bring up strong feelings or memories in most people, but this potential trigger is less obvious and therefore easily overlooked. Other elements you might notice include when the behaviour tends to occur or who tends to be involved. For example, transition times can be challenging for some children and they may express their anxiety by becoming disruptive. Or you might notice a young person who consistently expresses hostility to female carers, possibly reflecting repressed anger towards her mother or another female caregiver. As you tune in more, you will likely connect more with the feelings and experiences that the behaviour expresses. One final thing to notice – perhaps the most important thing – that will increase your effectiveness in working with pain-based behaviour is how *you* feel.

How you may feel

As previously mentioned, working with pain-based behaviour can provoke difficult and undesirable feelings. These might include anger, resentment, fear, helplessness, incompetence, hurt or embarrassment, and they often arise in combination with one another. Much of the time, these feelings are triggered naturally by the behaviour and the circumstances in which it happens. Additionally, you may be absorbing some of the unbearable feelings the child cannot contain. For example, if a child is defending against a sense of pervasive shame with angry, aggressive behaviour, in addition to anger, you may feel worthless, humiliated and hopeless as well. It is important to find supportive people and processes that help you to identify and process those feelings so that they do not become (or remain) uncontainable for you. Indeed, many carers have their own experiences of feeling uncontained (i.e. that the behaviour and their feelings about it become unmanageable). It is important that you have places to make sense of this and other aspects of working with pain-based behaviour, whether that be in supervision, team or carers' meetings or consultancy sessions.

You're going to get it wrong sometimes

If you are working with a child or group of children who have a lot of pain-based behaviour, you won't always be able to respond in a perfectly ideal way. Given the nature of pain-based behaviour, there's a very good chance that sometimes you'll have no idea what a 'good' response even looks like – not necessarily because of a lack of knowledge but because of how challenging it can be. The frequency and impact of it can feel (and be) relentless, and this makes it all the more difficult. Relative to the general population, you have chosen to go where most others fear to tread; but take heart, others have come before you and helped a child through similar dark valleys. Others will follow you as well.

While an ongoing commitment to do your best is necessary, it's also important to have good strategies in place (and to use them) when you do get it wrong. This is also part of doing your best. Supervision, team meetings, foster carers' groups and sessions with a consultant are all potentially good places to gently but honestly discuss and make sense of such occasions. How you handle it with the child or young person also warrants consideration. Many children and young people have little sense of how to repair relationships and they will be reliant on you to model this for them. It can be a very powerful experience to hear an adult say something like, 'You know, I'm really not happy with how I spoke to you this morning and I wish that I hadn't become so frustrated about what was happening.' Or 'I'm sorry. I could see you were really angry and it would be great if we could learn how to communicate better with each other when that sort of thing happens.' Statements like these not only model how to take responsibility when things go poorly, but how to share responsibility for making it better without inflicting blame on anyone. A child may need several experiences of this before she has the wherewithal to take even the first step towards holding herself accountable.

Counter-aggression

An understanding of **counter-aggression** can be very useful in helping carers to honestly reflect on their own practice and to make sense of some of the more challenging parts of it. The term counter-aggression refers to the aggressive thoughts, feelings and sometimes behaviours we experience as a result of someone else's aggression. Most of us have experienced counter-aggression in the face of a young person's pain-based behaviour. Indeed, feelings of aggression are a normal reaction to someone else's aggression. Nicholas Long, a well-published author who has written extensively about working with challenging behaviour, has argued that counter-aggression may even be a biological instinct that has helped human beings survive. Further work by him is included in the suggested further reading and resources at the end (Long 2004).

What might trigger a counter-aggressive reaction in you may be different from what would trigger it in someone else. Some common triggers include feeling physically threatened, a sense that our values or beliefs are being violated, or situations that provoke a feeling of helplessness, discouragement or loss of control. Situations or events that trigger unresolved issues or painful memories from our past can also cause a counter-aggressive reaction. People can often be unaware of their own counter-aggression or why it has been triggered. We may think that we are calm and fully in control, when actually our body language, tone of voice or facial expression conveys our aggressive feelings.

Pause for Reflection

What are some of the things that tend to trigger a sense of anger or aggression in you? How do you tend to react when these feelings get triggered? Could any of your reactions be a form of counter-aggression?

Counter-aggression clouds our thinking. Feelings of counter-aggression can trigger a biological response, not unlike the fight or flight response. When we feel threatened, our minds and bodies become focused on survival and our heart rate is increased. In the midst of this physical and emotional reaction our normal capacities to think and reflect often become overwhelmed or impaired. We may take decisions that are punitive and serve our own desire for control or retaliation when we are having a counter-aggressive reaction. It can be even harder to see our own passive-aggressive behaviour. In carers, passive-aggressive behaviour can take many different forms. Some examples include being slow to respond to a young person's request when there's not a good reason for delay, using cutting humour or being unreliable with a young person. Passive aggression is often a form of counter-aggression, and (like counter-aggression) people are usually unaware when they are behaving passive aggressively.

Whatever form it takes, counter-aggression makes us less effective in working with pain-based behaviour and is detrimental to building therapeutic relationships with young people. The first step in reducing its negative impact is to cultivate a firmly honest but gentle self-awareness about it. Acknowledging your feelings of counter-aggression can immediately diffuse some of their power and enable you to put them aside when in the midst of dealing with a young person's pain-based behaviour. You may need to remove yourself from the situation and say to a colleague, 'I am feeling so angry and part of me wants to retaliate.' Later, it will be important to reflect on, and talk about these thoughts and feelings, what they tell you about your tendencies and how they impact on your caregiving.

Reverting to old behaviours

Recovery and development aren't linear. That is, getting better at something or getting over something usually involves a long process of moving forward and moving back, testing out new strategies and reverting to old patterns until new skills, confidence and a new sense of self in relationship can be firmly established. Sometimes a return to old behaviours might be a regression back to something from an earlier developmental stage (as discussed in Chapter Two). This kind of regression can be triggered by changes, losses and transitions that may remind the child of previous losses. It can be frustrating and painful for carers when children revert back to old coping strategies or behaviours or regress back to behaviours more akin to an earlier developmental stage. It can also cause anger and indignation. So while you may have exercised the patience of a supreme being while going through a particularly rough patch with a child, you may be caught off guard when that child, after a period of improvement, returns to previous behaviours. You may take the behaviour personally or feel a strong sense of defeat. It's important to keep in mind that the child, too, may experience significant hopelessness during this time, and it may help you to know that reverting to old behaviours or regressing is a normal part of recovery and development. In fact, sometimes it is the periods of regression that really make it clear just how much progress has been made.

How you and others can help

It is important to always consider and, where possible, rule out physical causes of behaviour. Serious mental health issues and illnesses that cause physical pain may need to be diagnosed and treated medically. Other causes, including hunger, dehydration or fatigue, may be addressed more readily through your direct care.

While there is no formula for working with pain-based behaviour, there are some strategies that can help. Some of these have already been discussed in the chapter; these include remembering the emotional pain that often underlies 'challenging' behaviour; attending to the meaning that each person is making about what is happening and remembering that these meanings may well be very different; tuning into and actively managing your own triggers and counter-aggression; considering what you might be absorbing from the child; and firmly but gently using your own instances of less-than-ideal responding to model how to take and share responsibility.

Other strategies for intervening can range widely. On the least intrusive end of the spectrum, sometimes getting a child back on track can be as simple as a bit of eye contact and a smile. For others, it may be a matter of decreasing the physical distance between you – the sense of presence brought about by your closeness can help a child to feel that bit more in control of herself. Sometimes, rather than bolstering the child's inner controls through connection, giving a bit of space may be what's needed. This can be especially effective if you find yourself in a power struggle with a child or young person; if you have a colleague or partner-in-caring who can step in and take your place in a heated situation, all the better.

Sometimes, adults can use **star-charts** or other systems of points and levels to address behaviour. These can be really effective with some children, especially in relation to what we might think of as 'low grade' behaviours like tidying her bedroom or remembering to brush her teeth. These techniques work less well when the behaviour is feeling based. As discussed in Chapter Four, some children fundamentally do not believe that they deserve good things – even gold stars. Others will have such an underdeveloped sense of capability that they will see no point in even trying to achieve what is intended by these systems. In such cases, their lack of ability or deserving will be reinforced to them and the chart or system will be counterproductive. Even for children who do well with star-charts and **point-and-level systems**, the extrinsic nature of these approaches may not actually promote intrinsic characteristics such as empathy or respect for others.

For all children and young people, but especially for those who suffer from pervasive shame, it is important to convey care and remain emotionally available as much as possible when responding to pain-based behaviour. This can include making your own thoughts and feelings available to the child and showing genuine curiosity about hers. Much of the advice in relation to working with challenging behaviour stresses the importance of remaining calm. While this can be good advice, it must be handled with care because in the effort to stay calm, carers can sometimes shut down (or appear to shut down) emotionally. For a child who struggles with pervasive shame, this will be experienced, consciously or unconsciously, as rejection and/or abandonment. While we certainly would not advocate becoming escalated alongside the child, a degree of animation that reflects the child's but is at a more manageable level is more likely to be helpful (and possibly achievable).

Staying emotionally present and available in the face of pain-based behaviour does not mean becoming a pushover. It's important to convey firmness and a clear message. If a child picks up conflicting messages, subtly or overtly, it will cause confusion and likely escalate the situation. Children and young people need clear explanations pitched at a developmental level they can understand, and they need to learn how to negotiate. There are times, however, when things are not negotiable and this, too, needs to be conveyed with clarity and firmness. For example, a child's desire to stay up 10 minutes past normal bedtime to watch the end of a programme will be an opportunity to support the development of negotiation skills. Staying up 2 hours later on a school night to watch said programme will not likely be negotiable.

Setting limits on behaviour

While your initial reaction to pain-based behaviour may be a desire to make it stop, you will help the child more if your overall goals are to support the child to express herself in a less destructive or unacceptable manner, and to facilitate her development of responsibility for her choices. Gary Landreth, a play therapist, suggests a three-step approach in setting limits on destructive or otherwise unacceptable behaviour. While some of his advice is more suited to the special environment of play therapy sessions, his approach to setting limits is useful for wider practice in the life-space. First, acknowledge the child's desires and feelings. This is best done with an attitude of understanding and acceptance, and that acceptance should be completely directed at the child's feelings and desires. The second step is to state the limit, and this is best done with clarity and firmness. The third step is to offer acceptable alternatives.

Spotlight on Practice

Example of a carer using Landreth's three-step approach to setting limits.

Shirley is shouting and swearing at Jean.

Jean: 'Shirley, I can see you're really frustrated and you want me to know how angry you are'. (Acknowledgement of desires and feelings.)

Jean: 'I'm not here for being shouted and sworn at.' (Statement of the limit.)

Jean: 'We can talk about what's got you so upset, or you can go for a walk outside to burn off some steam. If you want, I can go with you.' (Offering of acceptable alternatives.)

Of course, this approach must be tailored to the specific child and situation. Some alternative choices won't be suitable, given your knowledge of the child, and you'll find your own way of acknowledging the child's feelings and desires in a way to ensure that she feels heard. These steps won't always work in all situations where a limit must be set, especially if there is an immediate danger and the limit must be stated first, but it's important to remember that when we refer to a limit 'working' we mean it's done in a way that supports the development of alternative means of expression and responsibility for one's choices. 'Working' doesn't necessarily mean the child stops the behaviour immediately.

In situations of serious, imminent harm, there may even be times where stating a limit isn't enough and you must state a directive or even physically intervene. Intervening physically may simply involve a hand on the shoulder to guide a young person away from a situation, or even positioning yourself in the way of the object of a child's aggression. Again, these types of intervention must be based on your knowledge of the child, her typical reactions and the demands of the particular situation. The most extreme form of physical intervention is usually referred to as physical restraint, and your employing organisation should have very specific policies and training related to its use (if its use is sanctioned at all). The use of physical restraint in the care of children and young people is complex and contentious, and in-depth coverage is beyond the scope of this book. Suffice to say that any form of physically holding a child against her will should only be done when there is serious imminent harm and there is no better way of establishing safety – by 'better', we mean no other way that is in the child's best interest (usually a less invasive form of intervention) and is possible in that given situation. Should you want further information, we have included details of a freely available guidance document about physically restraining children and young people at the end of this chapter.

When thinking about setting limits, it can be easy to get so caught up in the *how* that consideration of *whether* gets overlooked. Fritz Redl and David Wineman were seminal authors on working with children in alternative care settings and had interesting things to say about this (Redl and Wineman 1952). They suggest that the behaviour should be significant enough to warrant a limit in the first place. A short outburst of shouting and swearing is far less likely to require a limit than a prolonged, escalating episode of verbal abuse. Some behaviour should be permitted without interference, even if it makes you uncomfortable. Examples might include messiness while making a cake or being loud while playing. Sometimes behaviour may need to be tolerated as a part of the process of a child learning and developing, but you still convey it is not what you expect in the long run. For example, you may need to tolerate temper tantrums from a child who is developmentally 2 years old, even if she is chronologically 6. You can still, however, covey an optimistic attitude that, in time and with support, she will develop different ways of managing her frustration. And sometimes, a child needs to learn from the natural consequences of her actions. So a child who consistently provokes other children may need to experience what happens, rather than adults always intervening before the other children even have a chance to react. Simply the experience of another child's reaction, however, is not likely to be adequate and it will be important to support the child in making sense of the event.

In addition to issues of safety, other reasons for intervening may include: a child's need to be protected from guilt or embarrassment, and therefore diverted from mildly harmful or socially unacceptable actions; other children's needs not to be adversely affected by a child's behaviour; the need of all involved to experience the continuation of some activity that would otherwise by stopped by a child's behaviour; or the need to keep the physical environment in a reasonably pleasant condition.

If you do deem it necessary to set a limit and the child persists in breaking it, you may need to offer a final choice. This final choice is usually something like placing an item temporarily off limits if it is being misused, or requiring a child to leave the room. It should be logically related to what is going on and immediate to the situation. A choice of missing the football game the following week isn't the kind of final choice that is referred to here and is much more likely to be punitive in its impact. Returning to the example above where Shirley's shouting and swearing is continuing in an abusive and escalating fashion, Jean might say something like, 'Shirley, if you choose to continue to shout and swear at me, then our card game will be over for today.' Requiring a child to leave the room may be effective with some children, and may escalate the situation into a power struggle with others. In the most extreme situations, this can lead to physical restraint – often unnecessarily. If the goal is to promote alternative expression and the development of responsibility rather than to get the child to do what we want, then there are likely to be many times when we can instead remove ourselves from the situation and that might even be the final choice. It may seem counter-intuitive, but we will likely have a more developed capacity for removing ourselves from the situation than children will have. Whatever the case, you should only resort to offering a final choice after the child has had sufficient opportunity to choose an alternative way of expressing her feelings or meeting her desires, and the final choice should never be a punishment. Unless safety is being jeopardised, patience is required and at least a few attempts of the three steps outlined above.

The use of consequences

Sometimes, pre-designated consequences are established and used as part of the attempt to create a sense of predictability, structure and boundaries.

Spotlight on Practice

When Laura worked in one residential home, a great deal of time and effort went into creating fair and logical consequences and making sure they were imposed consistently. It seemed that no matter how hard they worked to make them clear and weave them into the fabric of every day, it never seemed to 'work'. For example, they debated a lot about what the consequence should be for running away. They were so busy trying to achieve consistency that they overlooked the vital importance of tailoring their responses to pain-based behaviour to the particular needs of each child in the given moment. As a result, it was harder for their responses to be relational. Everyone tried to follow a list of specific consequences for specific behaviours in an effort to reduce the reactive, punitive use of consequences. In the end, it was more often simply a move from a personal infliction of punishment to an impersonal infliction of it.

It might be hard to imagine working with pain-based behaviour without the use of consequences, and many will question whether this would even be a desirable state of affairs. Perhaps exploring what is meant by the term 'consequence' and how it is used with children is a good starting point in considering whether their use is a good thing. Consequence simply means the outcome or result of something else. So the consequence of taking a shower is that you get wet. Sometimes in care settings involving children, consequences are referred to 'natural and logical', and efforts are made to create such consequences in order to avoid punishments. A consequence that is deliberately imposed by an adult on a child is not a natural consequence, but it may be a logical one. Proportionate, logical consequences have a greater chance of being experienced as a limit rather than a punishment. So, for instance, if an adult removes a computer game from a child's room who is continuing to play it well past bedtime, this is not a natural consequence but it is a logical one. That said, what may be logical to us as adults may not be logical to a child, especially if she has experienced disruption to her development due to relational trauma.

Finally, if you are using a consequence, the way that you communicate it to the child is very important. Along with what we've already written about acceptance and understanding of feelings and desires, as well as being clear and firm, the underlying message must be rooted in your care for the child. So, in the previous example, the decision to take the computer game from the bedroom is likely rooted in your desire for her to get enough sleep and to have positive experiences at school the next day. You might say something like, 'I am taking the computer game so that you can get enough sleep to feel okay tomorrow. I know you have a harder time with things when you're tired. Most of us do.'

This is a very different message to, 'You know the consequences for playing your computer game after lights out. It's your own fault that I have to take it away.' The implicit message in the first illustration is that you care enough to step in and take charge; in the second, the implicit message is that the child deserves to have something taken away against her wishes.

Working to keep perspective

In order to respond helpfully to pain-based behaviour, it may be hard to avoid the temptation to make simplistic assumptions about what a child is experiencing based on surface behaviour. This is especially difficult with a child who uses aggression in what may appear to be a controlled manner (as opposed to the child who tends to lose control). On the surface, it may appear that she doesn't feel bad about her harmful behaviour, or worse, that she gets some satisfaction from it. This may or may not be the case, but either way, this is only on the surface. There will be all sorts of feelings and beliefs about herself and others, some of which may indeed be related to pervasive shame. Helping a young person begin to touch into and experience those deeper parts of herself is part of the process of developmental recovery. This will likely be threatening to the young person and will require your own persistence and a dogged commitment to knowing her fully. It can take a very long time, with repeated efforts on the part of skilled and caring adults, before a child can even begin the process of shifting out of her defences against shame. Try to remain hopeful and optimistic while also bringing patience and a long-term vision to the process.

Acknowledging and getting support when you have been hurt

If you have been on the receiving end of pain-based behaviour you may have been hurt, physically and/or emotionally. If the incident was very traumatic, you may still have vivid memories about it that occasionally intrude on your day-to-day life. In our work with carers we have often found that their hurts and traumas can be overlooked or brushed aside, as everyone is most concerned about the well-being of the child. While the well-being of the child should be paramount, we should not ignore or neglect the needs of carers. Just like the children in our care, we cannot thrive and develop if we do not feel a sense of safety and security. Traumatic experiences, where we have felt threatened or abused, may leave us with a deep sense of insecurity and anxiety. In order to heal and move on from these feelings we need support to understand what happened and we need our feelings and hurts to be heard and acknowledged. Some might feel it best to 'soldier on' or they may even feel angry at themselves for not being able to just 'get over it'. In our experience, such strategies inevitably backfire, and carers who neglect their own hurts may end up feeling burnt out or may develop more long-term health problems. Carers with unacknowledged or unsupported hurts may also find it much harder to respond calmly to the next incident of pain-based behaviour from the child. The sooner you seek support and advice to recover from the hurts you have experienced, the better for you and for the child.

Everyday things you might like to try

- *Try the three-step* approach to setting limits (outlined above):
  - acknowledge, with empathy, the child's desires and feelings with understanding and acceptance
  - clearly and firmly state the limit
  - offer acceptable alternatives.
- Lots of times, a child can be helped to redirect her behaviour without it becoming a limit-setting situation. Things to try short of limit setting might include:
  - distracting the child with something positive to help her get on track
  - using gentle humour
  - addressing the feeling or issue behind the behaviour
  - negotiating the negotiable
  - moving closer

○ giving space

○ identifying what the child is doing well and drawing attention to that.

- *Write some rules in partnership with the child.* This sets a good foundation for learning to negotiate, and establishing what is negotiable and what is non-negotiable.

- When the child is calm, *try reflecting with her about a recent pattern of behaviour.* The objective here is to develop her awareness and insight into what thoughts and feelings might trigger certain behaviours for her and the consequences of this behaviour. There are a *range of useful workbooks* that might help you do this work with the child (see 'Further reading and resources').

- *Talk to children about solutions and positive futures.* Many of the children we work with feel their problems and negative behaviours are the constant focus of attention. This must be very frustrating and boring. If you and the child are feeling very stuck with problems try to spend some time imagining how things might be without these problems. Here are some questions to get you started: 'What will you notice when the problem is better?', 'What will you be doing differently when the problem is better?', 'What will you be doing instead?', 'How will your parent/friends tell that things are going better?'

- Look for the *tangible* ways children tell us they are in pain, and *acknowledge and respond with nurture.* For example, the sting of a scraped knee can be given a gentle plaster, or a sore head can receive a warm cloth – alongside the acknowledgement 'You're really hurting' or 'That's really sore.' The importance of naming the pain is as important as the practical measures to treat it.

- Rather than dismiss behaviour as *'attention-seeking'*, consider what the child is communicating to you about her needs and feelings. Instead of withdrawing your attention or criticising the child, consider how you might support her development related to this behaviour. In cases of early experiences of neglect or unreliable caregiving, this may well mean lots of attention. In other cases, it may mean helping the child learn to entertain herself for short periods, or building her sense of being special or important.

  ○ Gently name the behaviour, without scorn or blame; for example, 'You're really worried we might forget to notice you.'

- Establish a regular practice of *remembering the circumstances* of the child coming into care and the related pain she has experienced. It is easy to lose the vividness of this pain in the busyness of the everyday, and it is hard to keep it in mind. When it becomes a somewhat regular topic of supervision, link worker meetings or team meetings, it becomes easier to bear.

Conclusion

The way that we think about behaviour will impact significantly on whether or not we respond helpfully to it. Information referring to pain-based behaviour, and understanding the issues that underlie it, is offered here in order to support you in that endeavour. Being firmly honest, yet also gentle in working with your own triggers will help you to be firm and gentle with the child or children you care for. The healing for the child will be in the cumulative impact of your everyday endeavour.

Further reading and resources

Anglin, J.P. (2002) *Pain, Normality, and the Struggle for Congruence: Reinterpreting Residential Child Care for Children and Youth.* New York: The Haworth Press.

Cavanagh-Johnson, T. (2005) *Understanding Children's Sexual Behaviors: What's Natural and Healthy.* South Pasadena, CA: Toni Cavanagh-Johnson.

Davidson, J., McCullough, D., Steckley, L. and Warren, T. (2005) *Holding Safely: A Guide for Residential Child Care Practitioners and Managers About Physically Restraining Children and Young People.* Glasgow: Scottish Institute of Residential Child Care.

Garfat, T. (2004) 'Meaning making and intervention in child and youth care practice.' *Scottish Journal of Residential Child Care, 3*, 1, 9–16.

Garfat, T., Fulcher, L., and Digney, J. (Eds.) (2013) *Making moments meaningful in child and youth care practice*. Cape Town: CYC-Net Press.

HandsOnScotland (2010) 'A Toolkit of Helpful Responses to Encourage Children and Young People's Emotional Wellbeing.' Available at: www.handsonscotland. co.uk/index.html (accessed 12 August 2015).

Landreth, G. (2002) *Play Therapy: The Art of the Relationship*. Hove: Brunner-Routledge.

Long, N.J. (2004) 'Why Adults Strike Back: Learned Behavior or Genetic Code?' *CYC-Online*. Available at: www.cyc-net.org/cyc-online/cycol-0104-long.html (accessed 12 August 2015).

Scottish Association for Mental Health (n.d.) 'Beyond Appearances: Experiences of Self-harm'. Available at: www.samh.org.uk/media/296244/full_report.pdf (accessed 12 August 2015).

Stallard, P. (2002) *Think Good-Feel Good: A Cognitive Behaviour Therapy Workbook for Children and Young People*. Chichester: John Wiley and Sons Ltd.

Whitehouse, E. and Pudney, W. (1998) *A Volcano in My Tummy: A Resource Book for Parents, Caregivers and Teachers*. Gabriola Island, Canada: New Society Publishers.

A range of short videos on parenting with non-violent communication are available on YouTube from the Non-Violent Communication Academy. See, for example:

www.youtube.com/watch?v=IQO7h9MNCqI

11

Bridge to the World

Introduction

John Donne, a famous English poet, once wrote that 'No man is an island, entire of itself'. This quote has often been repeated and will be a familiar saying for many of us. It has probably become a popular phrase because most of us would agree that it expresses a basic truth. People need each other. We are social creatures and for most of us, lack of contact and connection with other human beings makes us unhappy.

This chapter is about the basic need that children and young people have to develop a rich and rewarding social world. The networks that they develop with others are crucial to developing their resilience; indeed the stronger these networks are, the more likely they are to flourish and the more protected they will be from developing mental and physical health problems in later life.

In supportive caring families, parents take an active role in helping children to develop and sustain their social networks; this is something residential workers and foster carers should do too. This involves practical everyday things like encouraging friendships, facilitating sleep overs, cheering him on at sports and other social events. It also involves helping him to problem solve when things get difficult with friends, boyfriends and girlfriends, or teachers or other important adults. These parents help their children plan for the future and think about and learn about the roles they might take in the future. These parents encourage and nurture the child's talents, helping him to think about how he might develop these through college or university courses, voluntary work, internships and employment.

We have called this chapter 'Bridge to the World' because many children who enter the care system can find themselves cut off from networks or stuck within service-related networks that limit their inclusion into wider society. Carers can be a bridge to the wider world for children and young people, facilitating the development of social networks and peer relationships and modelling how this is done.

Drawing on relevant research and the experiences of carers and social workers, this chapter will examine the importance of peer relationships, social networks and social roles, and how carers can help the child to develop these. It answers these commonly asked questions:

- How can I help children develop and sustain friendships?

- How can I support children when they are having difficulties in their friendships or other relationships?

- How can I develop the children's social networks and help them feel they have meaningful place in the world?

The importance of social networks

A social network can be described as the connecting web of people in an individual's life and their interrelationships between one another. Social networks are important because of the social support that they can offer individuals; they are also important in shaping our identity. This means that we often think about ourselves and understand ourselves through our membership and association with others. Social support can include practical things like information and material resources as well as emotional support, validation of worth and help with 'problem solving'. Many of the things we learn about how to negotiate the social world are passed on through the people in our social networks including teachers, neighbours, family friends and peers.

Pause for Reflection

Think back to primary school. Who were the important people in your social world? What kind of support did they provide to you? How did your parent(s) or carer(s) help to nurture these relationships?

If we think back to our own childhoods and our social networks, they were probably closely linked to those of our families. Reflecting on her own upbringing, Autumn remembers how much support she received from some of her mother's female friends. Sometimes they were the ones she could talk to when it was difficult to talk to her mother about things like boys or friendship difficulties. By cultivating her own social network of caring female friends, Autumn's mother was also providing her daughter with an additional source of affection, advice and comfort.

Children and young people can clearly benefit from the social networks of their parents and extended family. However, some social networks are more supportive then others. One carer described having many friends and social networks but found them a burden, rather than a source of support. She found she was giving to others in her network all the time, but got little back. In order to look after herself and have enough energy for her family, she decided she needed to pull back from some of these relationships.

Social capital

Some theorists have used the term **social capital** to describe the strength of social networks between people and the amount of reciprocity and trust in these relationships. The term is helpful because it describes a kind of wealth that is not purely material. You may not have much money but if you have a lot of social capital it means that there is a richness to your relationships and social networks; you can draw on the resources of these networks and relationships to help you and your family. Social capital is not just about individuals and their networks; communities and organisations can also have more or less social capital depending on the amount of trust and reciprocity between the people and networks involved.

Spotlight on Practice

The Smith family had five children, two of whom were foster children, and very few financial resources; however, the Smiths had access to a lot of social capital. They lived in an area where many people lived a hand-to-mouth existence, surviving on benefits or low paid work. However, this community was rich in social capital. There was an active neighbourhood association and parent council at the school. The local authority had recently provided a new community centre, and parents had petitioned for the development of a skate park for the young people. This family had good relationships with the other families on their street, strong links to the local school through their involvement with the parent council and a supportive extended family who lived nearby. This allowed them to access resources such child care, advice and information, emotional support when things were hard and material support such as access to a washing machine when theirs was broken. This example illustrates how social capital is about reciprocity. This family was lucky to live in a community where people cared about each other and were prepared to share what they had and work together. This family was able to further enhance the social capital of their community by giving back as much as they received. Social capital flows from communities and organisations to individuals and their networks and back again.

Pause for Reflection

Take a moment to think about the communities and organisations in your life. What resources do you have access to through these communities and organisations? What do you feel you give to these communities or organisations? What do you get back in return? What might you do to develop the sense of reciprocity and trust in the communities and organisations you are involved with?

Eco-maps

In social work assessment **eco-maps** are a popular way of mapping a person's social networks and the quality of these relationships. People are asked to think about the people in their lives, how important these relationships are, and whether the relationship is a source of support or tension and difficulty. Below is an example of an eco-map for Maggie, a foster carer for Annie who is 18 months old. In this eco-map Maggie has highlighted the relationships that are supportive to her. Those closest to her in the map are most supportive and those less close to her are felt to be less supportive.

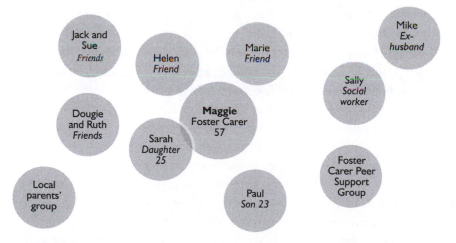

Figure 11.1 Eco-map for Maggie

Maggie's eco-gram shows that her strongest reciprocal relationships are with her daughter and her friends Helen and Marie. These are the people she feels she can rely on no matter what; they regularly spend time listening to each other and sharing advice and humour to lighten each other's stresses and burdens. These people are also really important in Annie's life. All three of them have spent time with Annie at Maggie's house just playing with her and, after undergoing police checks and a review from the social work department, Sarah has watched Annie on her own to give Maggie a break from time to time. Maggie has a wider network of friends like Dougie and Ruth and people from the Foster Carer Peer Support Group, who she sees less often but also finds supportive. In sharing her challenges as a carer in this group, she has helped to develop the Peer Support Group as a place where foster carers feel they can be honest about the challenges of the job.

This is only a brief overview of Maggie's social networks but it is clear that Maggie has a good deal of social support and that her relationships are generally characterised by reciprocity and trust. Maggie puts a lot of work into cultivating and maintaining these networks and makes it a priority to participate in groups that offer mutual support for parents and carers. In so doing, Maggie is maintaining and developing her social capital and enhancing the social capital of her community. Annie benefits from this in a number of ways. Through Maggie, Annie has access to a wide range of caring supportive adults who take an interest in her and her progress. These people send her birthday cards and spend time with her when visiting Maggie. Annie is gaining valuable insight into the social world by having the opportunity to engage with adults of different ages and genders. Maggie is also modelling for Annie how to conduct reciprocal, supportive relationships and is ensuring that Annie has more support as she grows and develops.

Not surprisingly, research shows that children's development is influenced by the amount of social capital in their community and family. Children's opportunities, choices, educational attainment and behaviour are all shaped by the amount of social capital within a child's family, school, peer group and larger community. Children and young people do better at school, are more likely to go on to employment, form more stable adult relationships and are generally healthier in mind and body when they have access to strong social networks characterised by trust and norms of reciprocity.

Peer relationships and friendships

> *The longing for interpersonal intimacy stays with every human being from infancy throughout life; and there is no human being who is not threatened by its loss…the human being is born with the need for contact and tenderness.*
> (Fromm-Reichmann 1959, p.3)

As the quotation above suggests, human beings seem to have an innate need to engage with others, share something of themselves and establish mutual understanding. As children grow, their capacity to understand the feelings and behaviours of others and their strategies for social engagement develop. As we explored in Chapter Two, child development is complex and there is a dynamic relationship between the innate capacities of the child and way that the environment supports or inhibits the development of those capacities. Social relationships and our need for belonging are driving forces in the process of development.

Developmental research suggests that children can begin to form friendships from as early as 2 years of age. These early friendships may involve more playing alongside one another (often described as parallel play) than playing together, but even very young children can begin to notice and engage with peers. As their cognitive capacities and their ability to understand the minds of others evolve, so does their style of play and engagement with peers. Children will move on from parallel to associative play, in which they begin to share materials or resources. By around the age of 5 most children are beginning to engage with cooperative play, in which they assign roles, take turns and work together. These and other developmental milestones are important in helping children to develop social networks.

For most children, peer relationships become much more important by the time they go to school and, in early childhood, friendships are often focused around shared activities and interests. As they move into late childhood and adolescence, peer relationships become increasingly important for young people. Their need for belonging also intensifies and young people may begin to search in a more deliberate way for a peer group that can help them to meet this need. Research has found that loneliness is most prevalent in adolescence. This is perhaps not surprising given that it is a significant time of change and transition for young people. While bonds with parents and carers remain important, most adolescents are beginning to focus more on peer relationships and many will experience their first sexual relationships. Young people's expectations about peer relationships also change in adolescence, as they seek greater intimacy, reciprocity, support and loyalty.

A key challenge in adolescence relates to the search for identity and autonomy. Adolescents have increasingly sophisticated capacities for abstract thought and reflection, and will be thinking more about what they believe and value and how they fit into the social structures that surround them. They will be likely to be feeling more responsible but also more separate, leading to a stronger need for peer affiliation and a greater vulnerability for loneliness. Although most people experience feelings of loneliness at some time in their lives, ongoing or chronic loneliness has been found to be correlated to poorer mental health and physical health.

The concept of loneliness is important because it highlights the significance of our perceptions of friendships and relationships. Studies of loneliness suggest that it is not the size of your social network or the number of friends that matter; what matters is how you feel about the quality of those relationships. Solitude or aloneness may not be a negative experience; however, if you are feeling bad about being alone and you are yearning for contact and connection, then you are lonely. If this becomes a chronic state, your mental and physical health is likely to deteriorate.

Pause for Reflection

Think back to your own adolescence. Who were your friends? How did you become friends? What did it mean to you to have these friends? How did they help you to negotiate the challenges you were facing at this time in your life?

What you may notice

As we have explored in previous chapters, children and young people's early relationship experiences with parents and other caregivers have a lasting impact on how they see themselves and how they relate to others. Children who have missed out on security, warmth and reciprocity in early relationships can find it more difficult to develop and maintain friendships and social networks as they grow and develop.

Carers and teachers may notice a range of difficulties for these children in engaging with, and relating to, peers, and building positive social networks. In order to protect themselves from the emotional pain of an unresponsive and rejecting parent who finds the child's emotional needs overwhelming and unacceptable, children will often develop coping strategies that include withdrawal and self-reliance. In adolescence these children may have few friends and be dismissive about the need for friends.

Spotlight on Practice

Lucy was raising significant concerns at school. The teachers described her as hostile and rejecting towards her peers, and described her attitude as 'arrogant' and 'aggressive'. In working with Lucy, the worker uncovered that Lucy's mother had a long-standing alcohol problem. Throughout her childhood Lucy had been on the receiving end of unpredictable parenting, which was at times rejecting and dismissive of her feelings and at other times overly intrusive. Lucy said she did not need friends and preferred to be alone. She would reject others in order to ensure they did not get the chance to reject her first.

Ben was another young man whose experiences of care had profoundly impacted on his relationships with peers. Ben's mother had suffered from depression and Ben had been moved around between lots of different relatives during his primary school years, during which time he was physically abused by an auntie's boyfriend. Ben had become friendly with a group of boys who were known to bully other children and had been shoplifting and vandalising property. Ben was desperate to maintain their friendship and was constantly pre-occupied with whether they would reject him. He was so desperate for approval and a sense of belonging that he was often willing to take huge risks in an attempt to please or impress his friends.

The experience of relationships was fraught with anxiety and uncertainty for both of these young people and they often felt lonely and rejected. Their strategies for engaging peers had developed from a place of insecurity and a fear of rejection. In both cases they had limited peer relationships and those that they did have were not particularly positive.

As we have already mentioned, social networks and peers can be very important in supporting identity development. As this need intensifies in adolescence the young person may want to seek out groups and networks that remind them of their family and where they believe they are 'from'. For example, Autumn has worked with a number of children who went through a phase of listening to a lot of rap and talking about being from 'the hood'. Although these children were from a white Scottish background, they identified with the idea that they came from a marginalised community and felt this music reflected something about their experience and roots. Race, culture and class can be important markers of identity for many of us, and having social networks that reflect and support this identity may be very important. Understanding this may help us to empathise with why young people are drawn to particular groups and networks.

What you may feel

As a parent or carer we want to feel proud of the children or young people we are looking after. When children struggle to engage with peers or build positive relationships with teachers or other important adults, we may feel very frustrated and embarrassed.

Spotlight on Practice

Nancy, a foster carer, was at her wits' end in working with an 8-year-old boy called Steve. Nancy had been working very hard to support Steve to develop positive relationships with children in his class at school by reaching out to fellow parents. However, every time there was birthday party or a social event at the school Steve would inevitably cause other children upset by being overly boisterous or demanding in his play. Nancy found herself becoming increasingly anxious and worked up before these events, anticipating some disaster or embarrassment and worrying about Steve's ever-diminishing chances of making a friend.

Through supervision and support Nancy began to reflect on how Steve might be feeling in social situations and realised that, just like her, he was feeling very anxious and wound up. He knew he was 'getting it wrong' with other children but didn't know what else to do. Reflecting on these feelings helped Nancy to empathise with Steve and to think about what kind of social situations he might find it easier to negotiate. Nancy began talking to Steve about his relationships at school and, over time, was able to begin to help him think about how other children might be feeling and establish some different approaches to engaging with them.

Peer relationships can cause parents and carers considerable worry, particularly when we are aware that children or young people are spending time with peers who are encouraging them to engage with risky behaviours like drug use or offending behaviour. Sometimes our first reaction may be to try and prevent young people from seeing particular peers. This is usually a counter-productive strategy. The first thing we need to do is to understand the young person's relationship to their peers from their perspective, including what they like about these young people and what they enjoy doing together. We should try to avoid jumping to conclusions about the motives or intentions of other young people. We should also remember that children may gravitate towards other children who have had similar experiences to them. For children and young people who have had very chaotic and abusive family experiences, finding a friend who can relate may be incredibly comforting.

We should work to develop a relationship with the young person's friends and the family of those friends. Providing activities that they will enjoy, that you can also take part in, will help to break down barriers and allow you to get to know these friends.

You may find it hard to like the friends the young person chooses, but in our experience, if you take the time to get to know them it will be easier for you to understand their relationship and why it is important to the young person. If you establish an open dialogue about their friendship group you can share your reflections and concerns in a way that is informed and less judgemental. It can help to remember just how desperately important it can feel in the teenage years to have the approval of others your own age. For many of the children we work with, years of neglect, abuse and loss make them even more desperate for approval and affection.

What you and others can do to help

Taking an interest and noticing who is important

The first thing you can do to help is to recognise just how important peer relationships and social networks are to children and young people's development. Positive peer relationships and friendships have been found to increase children's sense of well-being and increase their resilience in the face of adverse experiences such as loss and abuse. Social networks and social capital can enhance opportunities for learning and increase access to resources such as advice and material assistance.

Carers are a crucial resource for children and young people who are struggling to make friends or dealing with feelings of loneliness. Research has shown that parents who take an interest in their children's friendships and social networks and seek to monitor and provide age-appropriate control over these relationships can help children from developing affiliations with peers whose behaviours may be anti-social. Carers can also provide ongoing support and modelling to support their children's development of social skills. As young people begin to develop more intimate relationships and engage in sexual activity, carers' advice and support can be a protective factor against early sexual activity and teenage pregnancy.

A range of studies have shown that, although they may say otherwise sometimes, young people appreciate it when parents and carers take an interest in their world and their concerns. By being warm, open and communicative but not overly intrusive, engaged carers can be a sounding board to help children negotiate the confusing and, at times, upsetting world of friendships and relationships. This type of parenting is often described as authoritative (but not authoritarian) parenting and has shown to result in decreased risk-taking behaviours and greater self-esteem and well-being among adolescents. In this style of parenting the parent: is very warm and caring towards the child; seeks to exert positive control over the child with clear boundaries and consequences for behaviour; is communicative and models how to reason and negotiate; and has high expectations about behaviour and performance at school.

As we saw in the example of Maggie earlier in this chapter, carers can enhance the social networks and social capital of the children and young people they work with by developing and maintaining their own social networks and giving attention to the quality of these networks. However, parents and carers can and should take additional steps to support children to develop their own social networks and access to social capital. In early and middle childhood the key focus for this is school. Relationships with peers and teachers are of crucial importance to children's success in education and to their developing sense of themselves as socially competent and likeable people. In order to support relationships at school carers need to know what is going on at school. This means taking the time to build up relationships with teachers and understand what the dynamics of the class are, and how the teacher sees your child. It's also important to develop an understanding of how your child sees and experiences the teacher. Appreciating the work that teachers do is about saying 'thank you', but it is also about responding to requests for information and attending parent/teacher meetings. Research on children and young people in the care system has consistently shown that there can often be poor communication and engagement with schools on behalf of looked-after children, leading to poorer educational outcomes. Communicating and engaging with schools also sends a crucial message to children and young people about the importance of education.

Unfortunately many children in the care system have had a lack of continuity in their social networks. Many of the families of these children have moved a lot, experienced periods of homelessness, and have lived in communities characterised by poverty and a lack of social capital. While social capital does not rely solely on access to material resources, research suggests that many of the stresses and strains associated with living in poverty and in communities of deprivation make it more difficult for individuals to develop their social capital.

As carers we need to recognise that children and young people have often been asked to 'start over' with new schools and placements and that the cumulative impact of this can be very damaging for their confidence in developing relationships with peers and others. Providing children and young people with a sense of stability in their placement with you means that, in time, they will feel they have a secure base from which to build their social networks and relationships. It is also important to find ways to maintain important relationships from the past for children, even if they are at some geographical distance. With technology like video calls it should be possible to ensure these relationships are not lost, even if people are far away.

It is also important to take an interest in all of the relationships in a child or young person's life and try to keep up to date with how they are developing. Sometimes parents and carers feel that adolescents in particular become very closed when it comes to talking about friendships and other relationships. In our experience children and young people are more likely to share if they know you are really interested. It can help to provide them with regular, non-threatening opportunities to talk. Many carers say that the car is a good place for this, as young people often feel more able to open up when the focus is on the road and there's time to kill.

Children and young people also respond well to adults sharing stories from their own youth and childhood. Autumn remembers fondly her dad telling her about the trajectory of certain 'popular' kids at his school who thought high school was the be all and end all. It can be immensely reassuring to know a trusted adult went through similar struggles and came through it all right in the end.

Friends in care

Relationships with peers in the same residential unit or foster home can be a particularly tricky area of practice. As Ruth's own research showed, we can tend to frame peer relationships between children in residential units in primarily negative terms, assuming that they will be 'up to no good'. It is really important to remember that children and young people can be a very important source of support to each other. Being 'in care' can make you feel very different to other young people your age, and this shared experience of being different can bring young people in care closer to each other. Ruth found that when you spend time with young people you find that they offer many resources and much support to each other, even when they don't always bring out the best overall behaviour in each other. The important thing for adults to do is to be consistent about rules and boundaries, but also warm and understanding about the need for connection and friendship. This is not simple, particularly when you may have concerns about younger or more vulnerable young people being badly influenced or exploited by other young people. Work to understand the dynamic between the young people and talk to them about it and about the kind of unit they want to live in. They are more likely to buy into rules and boundaries that they have helped to create and, in our experience, if you ask them you will generally find they have very high standards for the behaviour of themselves and others.

New activities, new networks

We need to ensure that children are given a range of opportunities throughout their childhood to try new activities and engage with different groups of children and adults. In work with Lucy, described earlier in the chapter, a key turning point was getting her involved with a hip hop dance group. She found something she loved doing and could relate to some young people her own age through the activity, which was much easier than at school. As we also explored in Chapter Five, shared activities that involve working cooperatively or moving to a shared rhythm give us an immediate experience of getting in sync with others. This can be a powerful way of giving children an experience of connection to others, which they may never have had. Singing with others, passing a football back and forth, walking and dancing with others are all good examples of this. This physical experience of connection through shared activity can, over time, act in reparative ways. The young person has a direct experience of being with others that is facilitated by the activity; they don't have to think about it. With physical connection and a sense of shared purpose comes the chance that in time they may feel the emotional and psychological benefits of being able to connect to others, contribute to a collective experience and be appreciated by others for their contribution.

We can encourage and facilitate these new networks and interests by being willing to put in the time and effort to support and sustain them. We know many carers whose days are filled with taking children from one club or group to another, watching sports events, going to dance and music recitals, and organising parties and sleepovers. Managing the busy social calendars of happy, active young people is hard work but the rewards are amazing. One carer told us about the efforts she made to maintain Scottish country dancing lessons for a young man in her care:

> *He was so worried the classes would end when he moved placement and the classes were far away from where we lived. Getting him there every week was tricky and involved a lot of cooperation with other parents but we kept it going for him. He appreciated it so much and learned early on how much we cared about him. Seeing him win his first medal was priceless.*

Transitioning out of care

This work to engage young people in activities and education needs to be ongoing and is especially important as they begin to transition into independent living. Points of transition are vulnerable times, and children leaving the care system are at much greater risk of homelessness, imprisonment, unemployment and teenage pregnancy. We need to take the long view of young people's developing social networks and relationships and help them to think about and plan for the future.

Research has also found that most young people who leave the care system end up back in regular contact or living with family, even when there were significant issues of neglect and abuse. This suggests that these social networks remain important to most young people, even when they have been in care most of their life. Although these contacts may not last in the long term, it can be important to explore with young people the pull back to these networks and what they mean for the young person's sense of identity and belonging. Where possible, accessing some supports from throughcare and aftercare services or other family support agencies to engage with the family and prepare for these transitions can be very important to the success of these reconnections. Even if things don't work out in the way the young person hoped, we have found that young people really appreciate the support to explore these relationships and networks.

Protecting privacy and feelings

Many of the carers we have known can find it difficult to know how much to share with other professionals or other parents about the child they are caring for. The impulse to share information usually comes from a desire to help others understand and empathise with the child in your care. While you can and should be an advocate for the child, care is needed when you are considering sharing information about the child with others.

We find that it helps to think this through at the very beginning of a placement and discuss it with the child, his social worker and your supervisor. Questions for discussion could include: How will we explain to new friends why you are living with me?

What might be some of the good and bad things that could happen if we share information with others?

It is also be important to be clear about the legal basis for the child's care. What if any rights to consent for particular activities do parents retain? Make sure you talk to the social worker about this early on in the placement and write it down.

Generally there is much we can say about a child's needs without going into the specifics of his looked-after status and history. So for example: 'Linda has had a lot of changes over the last few years and she is still not very sure about where she will be living in the long term. He might not be very willing to engage at the moment until some of these things are settled. It would help if you could be understanding about this and do all the normal things you would do to make a new child in your class feel welcome.' Helping teachers or play group organisers to be sensitive around such issues can really help your child to settle into a new group. So, for example, if Mother's Day or other holidays are coming up it can be helpful to remind teachers and others not to make too many assumptions about the kids in their class and make activities as inclusive as possible. For instance, suggesting a 'thank you card for someone important to you' rather than assuming everyone will have a mother to write a card for.

It helps to keep in mind the child's feelings about being looked after away from his birth family and the shame and embarrassment that may go with this. Research with children in care has identified that many of them feel powerless and confused and want to know more about what is happening and why. It is important that we help children to feel a sense of security and control, and involving them in decisions about how information is presented and shared can be an important part of this work. Chapter Nine provides more examples of how to talk to children.

Spotlight on Practice

Autumn remembers working in a residential unit where a girl named Kelly was having a very difficult time. Her behaviour was often aggressive in the unit and she would often stay out all night going to parties and clubs, returning to the unit under the influence of drugs and alcohol. She always went out with a couple of female friends who went to her local school. On one occasion she brought one of the girls, Mia, back to the unit with her in the early hours of the morning. They were both coming down from taking speed and ecstasy and were thirsty, hungry and a bit disoriented. Instead of sending Mia away, the staff on shift invited them both in to have some breakfast and tea. That morning was the beginning of a relationship with Mia and a turning point in relations with Kelly. It turned out that Mia, although rebellious and a bit reckless, had a good relationship with her own parents and siblings, who were loving and supportive. The staff recognised Mia as someone who could help Kelly to develop a network outside the care system; they nurtured this friendship and got to know Mia's family. When Kelly moved on to independent living, Mia remained an important friend and a role model who encouraged her to attend classes at college and get a part-time job.

Children and young people with disabilities

If the child in your care has a learning disability or some other form of disability it may be particularly difficult to help him to develop relationships with peers and networks outside of services. Finding ways to widen his social world and become more included in society is really important. We have found that completing a MAP or PATH plan with a child or young person and the people that can support him is a powerful way of understanding the dreams and hopes of a person with a disability and starting to move towards them. A visual representation of the young person's goals and dreams is created, with long- and short-term goals identified and people enrolled to support the plan. For further reading about this approach see the end of the chapter.

Wherever possible seek out inclusive universal provision through schools and local community centres. A befriender might be able to help the child or young person access these opportunities for the first time and develop his confidence. Peer advocacy through organisations like People First might also help the young person to find a community where he feels accepted and understood, and we would encourage carers to research organisations in their local area that provide such support.

Everyday things you might like to try

- *Complete an eco-map* with the child or young person to help you better understand who he sees as important within his social network. It can be helpful to describe this in age-appropriate ways. For example, with younger children you might say, 'Let's imagine that we are drawing a map of your private universe. You are the most important person in the universe so we will draw you at the centre. Now we need to think about who else is important. Let's do the most important people first and put them close to you on the map so everyone can see how important they are.'

- *Get involved with your child's school.* Suggestions include: offering to support a planned school trip, helping with a school project or event, joining the parents' forum, volunteering to help in class. It is also important to respond to communications from the school and try to attend everything you are invited to as a parent including: parent's evenings, sports days, fetes, school plays and recitals.

- *Investigate local clubs and groups* that the child could attend. It helps to go along and check them out beforehand to see the dynamics of the group and meet staff. Think about how your child might fit into the existing group. All this background information will help you explain the group to the child.

- Persevere! *The child may need to try lots of different activities and groups* before he finds something he clicks with. Most children like to try different things and may go through phases, so be patient and encouraging.

- If there is a lack of something in your area that the child would like to do, like the Brownies or Scouts, *volunteer to set up a group and get the child involved* with running things.

- Talk with your child about how he wants to explain to other people who he lives with and why. He might need to do this a number of times and may want to have different answers for different people. You can help your child to *create a script* that he can use. This can be a great way of trying out different explanations or responses and can be a real window into letting you know how your child feels. Be careful not to create it for him. It's okay to wonder about what the likely impact might be of whatever he decides. Talk with him about what he would like you to say too.

- Before taking the child to a new activity make a checklist of things that he might find difficult, for example: lots of noise, strangers, waiting in line. Make a plan for how you will pre-empt these possible triggers. For example: bringing a snack, headphones and soothing music, pre-booking to avoid any waiting around. You might also like to try writing a Social Story for the child as discussed in Chapter Five.

- Set up a signal with the child so he can tell you if he is finding something stressful or difficult in a new situation, and have a plan with the child for what you will both do. For example: the child will touch his nose to tell you it is getting a bit much. You will then say to the dance teacher, 'Adam needs a break for a minute.'

- For older young people *help them to research college courses, voluntary work, jobs or apprentice schemes.* Be willing to take them along to check things out. We find that even older young people appreciate our support to do things like this and are much more likely to try something if we offer to take them there the first time.

Conclusion

Human beings are social creatures and have a profound need to connect with others and be understood. Relationships help us to learn and to develop a sense of identity and belonging, which is crucial to our self-esteem and well-being throughout life. Children and young people need help from adults to learn how to communicate in relationships and negotiate the social world. They need fierce advocates who will help them access activities and opportunities that enable them to meet new people, make friends and develop their social networks. They also need parents or carers who look after their own friendships and social networks, and model how to engage in healthy reciprocal relationships. It is important to remember how much your social world can impact on the child, for good or ill. With warmth and perseverance, you can be a bridge that supports the child or young person to develop the friendships and relationships that will sustain them in the wider world.

Further reading and resources

O'Connor, T.G. and Scott, S.B.C (2007) *Parenting and Outcomes for Children.* York: Joseph Rowntree Foundation/York Publishing Services Ltd.

Smith, M.K. (2009) 'Social capital.' *The Encyclopedia of Informal Education.* Available at: http://infed.org/mobi/social-capital (accessed 13 February 2015).

Stein, M. (2006) 'Research review: young people leaving care.' *Child and Family Social Work 11,* 273–279.

Parenting Across Scotland provides information on a range of free parenting classes including the Incredible Years courses. Go to:

www.parentingacrossscotland.org/info-for-families/resources/free-parenting-classes-and-courses.aspx

For information on the Incredible Years training and resources go to:

http://incredibleyears.com/about/incredible-years-series

www.kidsmatter.edu.au/families/about-friendship/making-friends/helping-children-learning-positive-friendship-skills

www.healthychildren.org/English/family-life/work-play/Pages/What-Parents-Can-Do-to-Support-Friendships.aspx

For further information on MAP and PATH planning go to:

www.helensandersonassociates.co.uk/person-centred-practice/maps

12

Conclusion

Feeling that we are beloved and that we belong are fundamental human needs. This book has explored these needs, what can happen when they go unmet and how we might create a home that nurtures recovery. Although this book has focused on children in a range of substitute care settings, we hope we have helped you to think about yourself too and to consider how much understanding can be achieved when you reflect on your own experiences and feelings and make use of these in your work with children.

Caring for children who have experienced abuse, neglect or other trauma, helping them to regain developmental ground and get on track towards a happy and fulfilled adulthood, can be extremely rewarding. It can also be difficult. The growing recognition of the complexity of the task can mislead us into thinking that counsellors or therapists are the ones who hold the keys to recovery. The home that you make for a child and the everyday care you give her are the most important things that will help her heal from past hurts. If you take nothing else from this book, we hope it is this.

Home is not just the building and furniture, and care isn't just practical tasks. The glue that holds it all together is the relationship you cultivate and grow together. Yet it is hard for many children and young people to be in an alternative home, however healing, and to accept your care. The formation and development of relationships can be fraught and threatening. Much of this book has been aimed at supporting your development of the knowledge, skills and ways of being necessary to address these challenges; it has also endeavoured to put into words and reflect back to you what you may already know and do well.

The power of the everyday to enhance development is another key theme running through this book. Much of the necessary knowledge, skills and ways of being for tapping into this power are the subjects of the previous chapters. Some focus inward on the self and the home, highlighting what is known about areas like food, touch, communication, pain-based behaviour and rhythms and routines. Others focus outwards, towards past and future memories and towards relationships beyond the home. Still others are more oriented towards underpinning knowledge about relationships and development themselves. Of course there are overlaps amongst all three. All of the chapters are aimed at bringing together knowing, doing and being in the service of healing and developmentally enhancing care.

The care and development of the self is the third key theme running through all of the chapters. 'Care for the carers' often comes at the end of books or training sessions, or is treated as a separate, stand-alone topic. Instead, we have woven a focus on the carer – her thoughts, feelings and needs – throughout the book. This can be difficult. You are not only being asked to put the child at the centre of your thoughts and efforts, but also to attend to yourself and the impact that self is having on the process at the very same time. In order to be able to do this, reflection and other forms of self-care are essential. Support from your employing organisation, as well as from your personal network of friends and family, is also necessary. Just like the children in your care, you have a need to feel 'beloved' and to have a sense of belonging.

In your desire to do your best for a child or young person, you may have felt daunted, unsure or even bewildered at times. We also imagine you will have felt motivated and optimistic about making a positive difference. Our experiences of writing this book have been similar: from the very beginning, we have been motivated by our desire to make a positive difference to your caring efforts, and therefore to the children you care for. We are optimistic about children and young people's resilience and developmental potential, and we are similarly optimistic about the restorative power of good care. But we also felt daunted and unsure, and sometimes even bewildered. It has been important to us to get it right.

In writing this book, we wanted to acknowledge the difficulties and celebrate the magic of healing care. We wanted to validate the great importance of the work you do, to encourage and even inspire you to keep going when it's hard. We wanted to name some of the common feelings and experiences carers encounter as reassurance that you're not alone, that sometimes you won't get it right, and that that's okay. We hope we have succeeded and that this book fortifies you in your efforts to create a healing home.

Glossary

Absorption means taking in the emotions of another and can be thought of as receiving the unconscious communication of that person or group of people.

Active cognitive processing is the process of thinking that brings the emotional content into consciousness and names it, making it thinkable, 'speakable' and more manageable.

Ambiguous loss is when a loss is unacknowledged or lacks finality, therefore complicating the grieving process. For example, the grief of a child who has been abandoned by a parent will be complicated by hopes or even expectations of the parent's return.

Anchor points are a source of security or stability. For some people a predictable routine at certain points in the day can provide an anchor point; they know what to expect and can deal with other things with more confidence. Objects or people may also provide anchor points.

Attachment theory helps to explain why close relationships, especially at the start of life, are centrally important for human development, especially the ability to manage impulses and emotions, to learn to be in other relationships. It stresses that from infancy, how an infant's stress and distress is noticed and responded to has a significant impact on how he goes on to view him and the world around him. Attachment theory goes on to argue that this pattern of relationship experience can influence the ways in which future relationships are experienced.

Calm receptiveness means being open to the emotional communication of another without becoming overwhelmed or agitated.

Co-regulation refers to the ways in which our thoughts and feelings are managed (or not) by the responses of others (in this context). It suggests that communication is a continuous and dynamic process, influenced and shaped by all those involved.

Conscious refers to those parts of our experience that we are directly aware of.

Containment happens when unmanageable feelings and experiences of one or more people are absorbed and understood by another who 'gives them back' in a more manageable form – making them more containable. For this to be possible, the person who is absorbing them must not become overwhelmed by them.

Counter-aggression refers to the aggressive thoughts, feelings and sometimes behaviours that are experienced as a result of someone else's aggression.

Eco-maps are a simple visual assessment tool used to highlight relationships between a child or adult and their family, friends and other people in their social network.

Empathic acknowledgement is a form of communication that conveys understanding of the emotional experience of another other person. Absorption of that other person's emotions enables empathic acknowledgement.

Hyper-arousal is a state of increased physical, mental or emotional tension which is often associated with post-traumatic stress disorder

(PTSD). Being in a state of hyper-arousal can involve a constantly feeling 'on edge' or anxious, finding it difficult to relax, having a heightened awareness of threats, being easily startled, having difficulty sleeping and being unable to concentrate.

Hyper-vigilance is a state of perpetual vigilance or watchfulness, associated with post-traumatic stress disorder (PTSD) and trauma. Those in a state of hyper-vigilance are continually scanning their environment for potential threats, will feel tense and 'on guard' most of the time and will find it very difficult to relax.

Inner world is a way of referring to the overall existence and experience inside a person, including thoughts, feelings, beliefs, fantasies, dreams, hopes and memories.

Intensive Interaction is an approach to teaching the pre-speech fundamentals of communication to children and adults who have severe learning difficulties and/or autism and are still at an early stage of communication development. The teacher responds to and joins in with the behaviour of the learner. Through this process the fundamentals of communication are gradually rehearsed and learnt in a free-flow manner.

Internal working model is a mental blueprint for how relationships work, including how the self is and should be and how others are and should be. It is formed from early experiences of care, although other experiences throughout the lifespan can influence it. All people have one and it is usually something we are not conscious of.

Memory box is a term often used to describe a collection of objects which hold significance for a person. The objects are chosen to represent and promote memories of a person, place or time.

Mindfulness is a mind-body based approach to helping people to develop awareness of and better manage their thoughts and feelings. Mindfulness exercises such as meditation, breathing and yoga are intended to help people to pay more attention to the present moment and become more aware of their thoughts, feelings and body sensations. This awareness can help people to feel less overwhelmed and can improve concentration.

Passive aggression refers to subtle and often unconscious expressions of hostility or defiance.

Pervasive shame refers to a fundamental sense of being worthless, blameworthy and bad. People tend to develop pervasive shame as a result of very early childhood experiences of repeatedly being left with feelings of shame.

Picture Exchange Communication Systems is a tool for supporting children with communication and learning disabilities to express basic desires (for objects).

Point-and-level systems are a behavioural programme of intervention that involves children or young people earning points in order to advance to higher levels that involve greater freedoms and other rewards.

Projection happens when feelings that are too uncomfortable are unconsciously put onto another, sometimes by seeing that feeling in the other person and sometimes by getting that other person to feel that feeling.

Received communication refers to the emotions one person absorbs from another. These emotions are often conveyed unconsciously and can also be absorbed unconsciously.

Reflective parenting is an approach to parenting which requires us to take regular time out to think deeply about our parenting and to consider our emotions, experiences, actions and responses. By doing this regularly we will enhance opportunities to learn from our experience and plan for future challenges and opportunities.

Regression is a term that has its origins in psychodynamic thinking. It is used to describe how people sometimes unconsciously protect themselves, most often at times of anxiety. Regression involves an unconscious return to earlier developmental behaviours and beliefs.

Resilience is the phenomenon of developing well or even thriving under adverse circumstances.

Sensory memories is a term that refers to smells, sounds, bodily feelings or touch which represent a person, experience or place. It may be that such memories are powerfully felt but not necessarily accompanied by a picture or 'story' memory. Rather a smell triggers a feeling which has significance because of a past event.

Social capital is a term (in this context) used to describe the strength of social networks between people and the amount of reciprocity and trust in these relationships.

Social Stories are an approach developed initially to teach social skills to people with autism. Created by Carol Gray in 1991 this approach uses short descriptions of a particular situation, event or activity, which includes specific information about what to expect in that situation and why.

Stage theories are theoretical approaches to understanding human development share a conceptual starting point which is that human life can be considered in distinct stages, each of which involves the demonstration of particular behaviours.

Star-charts are a form of documenting a child's behaviour over time as an incentive for positive change. The 'star' in star-charts refers to star stickers, but a variety of stickers or images might be used.

Symbolic containment happens through the use of objects or indirect acts that help make unmanageable feelings more manageable.

Talking Mats are a visual communication system developed to aid those with communication difficulties to communicate effectively about things that matter to them.

Total Communication Environment is an environment which uses forms of communication that involve many of the senses (i.e. not just hearing) and are tailored to the communication needs of those who are in it.

Transition is a process or period of changing from one state or condition to another. Transitions can be triggered by developmental changes, such as puberty, or by particular events or experiences, such as going to a new school.

Unconscious processes are those which we are not aware of, but nevertheless are still present in our minds. These might include beliefs, feelings, memories or motivations.

Bibliography

Aldridge, J. and Becker, S. (2003) *Children Caring for Parents with Mental Illness: Perspectives of Young Carers, Parents and Professionals.* Bristol: The Policy Press.

Anglin, J.P. (2002) *Pain, Normality, and the Struggle for Congruence: Reinterpreting Residential Child Care for Children and Youth.* New York: The Haworth Press.

Attwood, T. (2002) *Why Does Chris Do That? Some Suggestions Regarding the Cause and Management of the Unusual Behaviour of Children and Adults with Autism and Asperger Syndrome.* London: The National Autistic Society.

Barton, S., Gonzalez, R. and Tomlinson, P. (2012) *Therapeutic Residential Child Care for Children and Young People: An Attachment and Trauma-Informed Model for Practice.* London: Jessica Kingsley Publishers.

Baumrind, D. (1978) 'Parental disciplinary patterns and social competence in children.' *Youth and Society 9,* 239–276.

Bee, H. and Boyd, D. (2013) *The Developing Child,* 13th edition. New York: Pearson.

Belle, D. (ed.) (1989) *Children's Social Networks and Social Supports.* Chichester: John Wiley and Sons.

Bion, W.R. (1962) *Learning from Experience.* London: Karnac.

Booth, P.B. and Jernberg, A.M. (2010) *Theraplay: Helping Parents and Children Build Better Relationships through Attachment Based Play.* San Francisco, CA: Jossey-Boss.

Brennan, T. (1982) 'Loneliness at Adolescence.' In L.A. Peplau and D. Perlman (eds) *Loneliness: A Sourcebook of Current Theory, Research and Therapy.* New York: Wiley.

Brown, B.B., Mounts, N., Lamborn, S.D. and Steinberg, L. (1993) 'Parenting practices and peer group affiliation in adolescence.' *Child Development 64,* 467–482.

Cairns, K. (2002) *Attachment, Trauma and Resilience: Therapeutic Caring for Children.* London: BAAF.

Cavanagh-Johnson, T. (2005) *Understanding Children's Sexual Behaviors: What's Natural and Healthy*. South Pasadena, CA: Toni Cavanagh-Johnson.

Chan, T.W. and Koo, A. (2011) 'Parenting style and outcomes in the UK.' *European Sociological Review 27*, 3, 385–399.

Cocker, C. and Allain, L. (2013) *Social Work with Looked after Children*, Second edition. London: Sage/Learning Matters.

Daniel, B., Wassell, S. and Gilligan, R. (2010) *Child Development for Child Care and Protection Workers*, Second edition. London: Jessica Kingsley Publishers.

Davidson, J., McCullough, D., Steckley, L. and Warren, T. (2005) *Holding Safely: A Guide for Residential Child Care Practitioners and Managers About Physically Restraining Children and Young People*. Glasgow: Scottish Institute of Residential Child Care.

Douglas, H. (2007) *Containment and Reciprocity: Integrating Psychoanalytic Theory and Child Development Research for Work with Children*. Hove: Routledge.

Emond, R. (2012) 'Longing to belong: Children in residential care and their experiences of peer relationships at school and in the children's home.' *Child and Family Social Work 19*, 2, 194–202.

Emond, R., McIntosh, I. and Puch, S. (2013) 'Food and feelings in residential childcare.' *British Journal of Social Work 43*, 2, 1–17.

Erikson, E.H. (1963) *Childhood and Society*, 2nd edition. New York: Norton.

Faber, A. and Mazlish, E. (2013) *How to Talk So Kids Will Listen and Listen So Kids Will Talk*. New York: Avon Books.

Fahlberg, V. (2012) *A Child's Journey through Placement*. London: Jessica Kingsley Publishers.

Fairbairn, W.R.D. (1952) *Psychoanalytic Studies of the Personality*. New York: Brunner-Routledge.

Field, T. (2014) *Touch*, 2nd edition. Cambridge, MA: The MIT Press.

Fiese, B.H., Tomcho, T.J., Douglas, M., Josephs, K., Poltrock, S. and Baker, T. (2002) 'A review of 50 years of research on naturally occurring family routines and rituals: Cause for celebration?.' *Journal of Family Psychology 16*, 4, 381–390.

Fromm-Reichmann, F. (1959) 'Loneliness.' *Psychiatry: Journal for the Study of Interpersonal Processes 22*, 1–15.

Gerhardt, S. (2004) *Why Love Matters: How Affection Shapes a Baby's Brain*. Hove: Brunner-Routledge.

Gilligan, R. (2001) *Promoting Resilience: A Resource Guide on Working with Children in the Care System*. London: British Agencies for Adoption and Fostering.

Golding, K.S. and Hughes, D.A. (2012) *Creating Loving Attachments*. London: Jessica Kingsley Publishers.

HandsOnScotland (2010) 'A Toolkit of Helpful Responses to Encourage Children and Young People's Emotional Wellbeing.' Available at: www.handsonscotland.co.uk/index.html (accessed 12 August 2015).

Happer, H., McCreadie, J. and Aldgate, J. (2006) 'Celebrating Success: What Helps Looked after Children Succeed.' Edinburgh: Social Work Inspection Agency. Available at: www.scotland.gov.uk/Resource/Doc/129024/0030718.pdf (accessed 12 August 2015).

Harms, L. (2005) *Understanding Human Development: A Multidimensional Approach*. Oxford: Oxford University Press.

Heinrich, L.M. and Gullone, E. (2006) 'The clinical significance of loneliness: A literature review.' *Clinical Psychology Review 26*, 695–718.

Hill, M., Stafford, A., Seaman, P., Ross, N. and Daniel, B. (2007) 'Parenting and Resilience.' Glasgow: Joseph Rowntree Foundation. Available at: www.jrf.org. uk/sites/files/jrf/parenting-resilience-children.pdf (accessed 12 August 2015).

Ironside, L. (2004) 'Living a provisional existence: Thinking about foster carers and the emotional containment of children placed in their care.' *Adoption and Fostering 28*, 4, 39–49.

Keenan, C. (2002) 'Working within the Lifespace.' In J. Lishman (ed.) *Handbook of Theory for Practice Teachers in Social Work*. London: Jessica Kingsley Publishers.

Kroll, B. (2004) 'Living with an elephant: Growing up with parental substance misuse.' *Child and Family Social Work 9*, 129–140.

Landreth, G. (2002) *Play Therapy: The Art of the Relationship*. Hove: Brunner-Routledge.

Long, N.J. (2004) 'Why Adults Strike Back: Learned Behavior or Genetic Code?' *CYC-Online*. Available at: www.cyc-net.org/cyc-online/cycol-0104-long.html (accessed 12 August 2015).

Maier, H. (1992) 'Rhythmicity: A powerful force for experiencing unity and personal connections.' *Journal of Child and Youth Care Work 8*, 7–13.

Malchiodi, C.A. (ed.) (2015) *Creative Interventions with Traumatized Children*. London: The Guildord Press.

Miller, B.C., Benson, B. and Galbraith, K.A. (2001) 'Family relationships and adolescent pregnancy risk: A research synthesis.' *Developmental Review 21*, 1–38.

Milner, J. and Bateman, J. (2011) *Working with Children and Teenagers Using Solution Focused Approaches*. London: Jessica Kingsley Publishers.

O'Connor, T.G. and Scott, S.B.C. (2007) *Parenting and Outcomes for Children*. York: Joseph Rowntree Foundation/York Publishing Services Ltd.

Perry, B. (2009) 'Hope Springs Eternal.' *CYC-Online* 123, May. Available at: www. cyc-net.org/cyc-online/cyconline-may2009-perry.html (accessed 30 September 2015).

Perry, B.D. and Szalavitz, M. (2004) *The Boy Who Was Raised as a Dog: And Other Stories from a Child Psychiatrist's Notebook*. New York: Basic Books.

Phelan, J. (2008) 'Building Developmental Capacities: A Developmentally Responsible Approach to Child and Youth Care Intervention.' In G.L. Bellefeuille and F. Ricks (eds) *Standing on the Precipice: Inquiry into the Creative Potential of Child and Youth Care Work*. Alberta: MacEwan Press.

Punch, S., Dorrer, N., Emond, R. and McIntosh, I. (2009) *Food Practices in Residential Children's Homes: The Views and Experiences of Staff and Children. A Resource Handbook for Reflection*. Stirling: University of Stirling.

Rae, T. (2007) *Dealing with Feelings*. London: Sage.

Redl, F. and Wineman, D. (1952) *Controls from Within: Techniques for the Treatment of the Aggressive Child*. New York: The Free Press.

Rees, J. (2009) *Life Story Books for Adopted Children: A Family Friendly Approach*. London: Jessica Kingsley Publishers.

Roesch-Marsh, A. (2012) *Behaviour as communication: Understanding the needs of neglected and abused adolescents*. Stirling: WithScotland.

Roesch-Marsh, A. (2012) 'Out of Control':Making Sense of the Behaviour of Young People Referred to Secure Accommodation.' *British Journal of Social Work*, doi: 10.1093/bjsw/bcs102.

Roesch-Marsh, A. (2014) 'Risk assessment and secure accommodation decision making in Scotland: Taking account of gender?' *Child Abuse Review, 23*, 3, 214–226.

Roffey, S. (ed.) (2012) *Positive Relationships: Evidence Based Practice Across the World.* London: Springer.

Rose, R. and Philpot, T. (2004) *The Child's Own Story: Life Story Work with Traumatized Children.* London: Jessica Kingsley Publishers.

Rosenberg, M.B. (2005) *Raising Children Compassionately: Parenting the Non-Violent Communication Way.* Encinitas, CA: PuddleDancer Press.

Ruch, G. (2007) 'Reflective practice in contemporary child-care social work: The role of containment.' *British Journal of Social Work 37*, 659–680.

Ruch, G. (2008) 'Developing "Containing Contexts" for the Promotion of Effective Work: The Challenge for Organisations.' In B. Luckock and M. Lefevre (eds) *Direct Work: Social Work with Children and Young People in Care.* London: British Association for Adoption and Fostering.

Scottish Association for Mental Health (n.d.) 'Beyond Appearances: Experiences of Self-Harm.' Available at: www.samh.org.uk/media/296244/full_report.pdf (accessed 12 August 2015).

Slatcher, C. (2011) 'Supporting Children Who Have a Parent with a Mental Illness: Information for Professionals.' Hampshire: The Children's Society. Available at: www.youngcarer.com/sites/default/files/mental_illness_booklet_2011_2nd. pdf (accessed 12 August 2015).

Smith, M.K. (2009) 'Social Capital.' *The Encyclopedia of Informal Education.* Available at: http://infed.org/mobi/social-capital/ (accessed 12 August 2015).

Stallard, P. (2002) *Think Good–Feel Good: A Cognitive Behaviour Therapy Workbook for Children and Young People.* Chichester: John Wiley and Sons Ltd.

Stallard, P., Norman, P., Huline-Dickens, S., Salter, E. and Cribb, J. (2004) 'The effects of parental mental illness upon children: A descriptive study of the views of parents and children.' *Clinical Child Psychology and Psychiatry 9*, 1, 39–52.

Steckley, L. (2010) 'Containment and holding environments: Understanding and reducing physical restraint in residential child care.' *Children and Youth Services Review 32*, 1, 120–128.

Steckley, L. (2010–2011) 'Constrained, Contained or Falling to Pieces?'; 'Containing the Containers: Staff Containment Needs in Residential Child Care'; and 'Containing the Containers II: The Provision of Containing Processes for Staff in Residential Child Care.' *CYC-Online: The International Child and Youth Care On-Line Journal*, November and December 2010; March 2011. Available at: www.cyc-net.org/cyc-online/cyconline-nov2010-steckley.html; www.cyc-net.org/cyc-online/cyconline-dec2010-steckley.html; and www.cyc-net.org/cyc-online/mar2011.pdf#page=59 (all accessed 7 August 2015).

Steckley, L. (2012) 'Touch, physical restraint and therapeutic containment in residential child care.' *British Journal of Social Work 42*, 3, 537–555.

Stein, M. (2006) 'Research review: Young people leaving care.' *Child and Family Social Work 11*, 273–279.

Szalavitz, M. and Perry, B.D. (2010) *Born for Love: Why Empathy Is Essential – and Endangered.* London: Harper.

Tait, A. and Wosu, H. (2013) *Direct Work with Vulnerable Children: Playful Activities and Strategies for Communication.* London: Jessica Kingsley Publishers.

Tomlinson, P. (2008) 'Assessing the needs of traumatized children to improve outcomes.' *Journal of Social Work Practice 22,* 3, 359–374.

Van Gulden, H. (1995) *Real Parents, Real Children: Parenting the Adopted Child.* New York: Crossroad Publishing Co.

Warman, A. (1990) *Recipes for Fostering: Sharing Food and Stories.* London: BAAF.

West, J. (1996) *Child Centred Play Therapy.* London: Hodder Education.

Whitehouse, E. and Pudney, W. (1998) *A Volcano in My Tummy: A Resource Book for Parents, Caregivers and Teachers.* Gabriola Island, Canada: New Society Publishers.

Whitwell, J. (1990) 'The Importance of Food in Relation to the Treatment of Deprived and Disturbed Children in Care.' Available at: www.johnwhitwell. co.uk/index.php/the-importance-of-food-in-relation-to-the-treatment-of-deprived-and-disturbed-children-in-care (accessed 12 August 2015).

Wilson, C. (2013) 'A different language: Implementing the total communication approach. *Scottish Journal of Residential Child Care 12,* 1, 34–45.

Wilson, P. and Long, I. (2008) *The Big Book of Blob Feelings.* London: Speechmark Publishing Ltd.

Acknowledgements

So many people have supported us in the writing of this book. While there isn't space to acknowledge all of those who have aided the development of our thinking and practice over the years, we would like to thank some people who directly contributed to our efforts. Our book is better as a result. In the final analysis, however, the responsibility for any errors or omissions lies with us.

For providing us with feedback on final draft chapters, we thank Melissa Bennett, Kimberley Best, Nicola Butt, Elizabeth Clark, Phil Coady, Graham Currie, Norah Grubb, Jaime Lundrigan, Tracey McQuillan, Paul Murray, Crystal Soper, Heather Storrier and Lesley Young. We are grateful that you took time from your direct caring duties to let us know whether they did the job. For organising residential and foster carers to give us feedback, thanks to Sandra Howden and Heather Modlin. For their dissertation research as described in Chapter Ten, we thank Susan Ainscough, Eileen Scott and Roisin Petticrew. For discussing her field work towards her upcoming PhD, we thank Lisa Warwick. Finally, for feedback on an earlier draft of Chapter Four, thanks to Patrick Tomlinson, and for such insightful comments on the full manuscript we are very grateful to Irene Stevens. We were struck by the readiness of all our reviewers to share their own, often deeply moving, views and accounts. We have learned a great deal as a result.

We are so grateful to Stephen Jones at Jessica Kingsley Publishers for trusting that we would finish this book and leaving us to just get on with it, and to the team at Jessica Kingsley Publishers for their support and guidance through the process.

The experience of writing this book has been hugely enjoyable not least because we have so enjoyed each other's company, wisdom, humour and tact. As we have argued throughout this book, there has to be care for the carers. To that end, we are indebted to those who have cared for us both at home and at work.

Laura would like to thank her family for patiently tolerating her periods of not being in touch due to working on the book, and her partner, Andrew, for putting up with her long nights and weekends in front of the computer. She also gives thanks to those friends and colleagues who have been such fantastic sounding boards, helping her think through various aspects of the book, and to her students who are continually a source of learning and inspiration. Finally, she would like to thank Rowena Murray for developing the model of structured writing retreat, and Liz, Andrew and the wonderful staff at the Black Bull in Gartmore for so capably hosting them. You have all made this possible.

Ruth has had great fun writing this book and returning to talk and think with previous children, carers and staff with whom she has worked. Thanks to them for continuing to remind her of how transformative love and care can be. Special thanks go to the staff at Family Change for their wisdom and passion for therapeutic work; to colleagues at the University of Stirling for their support and inspiration; to the Food for Thought team, who encouraged the use of food to be included in the book; to friends who talked and laughed about other things in life; to Helen and Willie Emond for all the top notch childcare and emotional support, and to Rudi for making every day the best adventure a person could have.

Autumn would like to thank the many courageous, clever, fun, feisty and fearless children and young people she has worked with over the years. They have taught her so much about the strength of the human spirit and our capacity to connect to one another.

She would like to thank many of the wonderful residential workers, social workers, foster carers and parents she has known and learned from. Their willingness to keep their hearts open in the face of so much hurt is an ongoing source of inspiration for her writing and her teaching. Autumn would also like to thank Edward for his partnership, friendship and love, and Alice for being the brightest light in her life.

Above all, the authors would wish to thank all of those children, foster carers, residential workers, social workers and managers who played a part in the stories and experiences contained in this book. We have learned a great deal from being allowed to sit alongside you for at least part of your journey and continue to be inspired by your bravery, passion and willingness to keep trying.

Index